AF599586

PRAISE FOR

MINE *Angels* ROUND ABOUT YOU

"Every future, current, and former missionary and their families and friends should read the book. The author does a great job documenting that the Lord loves His children as much today as He did in ancient times."

—FRANCIS W. "BUTCH" CASH

(Retired chairman and CEO of two Fortune 500 companies. He also served earlier as president of the Marriott Service Group and has presided over several other successful companies.)

"This book brought the mission field back so forcefully. The great power that drives the Lord's work is indeed invisible to the unbelieving. We reflect often on our own mission experience, and your accounts certainly remind us of many of our own experiences."

—NOEL B. REYNOLDS

(Author, emeritus professor of political science, chaired Dept. of Philosophy, twice served as associate academic vice president of Brigham Young University, former director of the Foundation for Ancient Research and Mormon Studies and executive director of the Neal A. Maxwell Institute for Religious Scholarship; former president of Mount Tipanogos Utah Temple and former president of the Florida Fort Lauderdale Mission.)

"I very much enjoyed reading your book and shared a few of your stories with our neighbors, one of whom had presided over a mission in Korea. Many stories were truly inspirational and reminded me of some of our experiences. Even though your experiences were different, it was like a trip down memory lane and reminded me how much Heavenly Father cares about all of His children and is willing to be involved in blessing our lives. You know my professional background has focused on trying to characterize uncertainty. I returned from our mission with a strong testimony that far fewer events in life are random than I'd previously thought.

"Your organization and presentation made your book very readable. I could go on and on enumerating your experiences that touched my heart. The story of dreams and numerous instances of following spiritual promptings are great reminders that miracles still take place."

—JAMES B. MCDONALD

(Author, Clayne L. Pope professor of economics at BYU, world-renowned econometrician, former president of California Anaheim Mission, stake patriarch, emeritus member of Fifth Quorum of Seventy.)

"I wish I had read this book before serving my own mission. I learned much of its lessons from the scriptures and the Spirit, but it would have helped enormously to know contemporary examples of faith and what was possible in missionary service. It is a reminder of the power of recording and relating our experiences with divinity. It is also a testament to the fact that God and His angels weren't just involved in the lives of those we read about in the scriptures and in the journals of Mormon pioneers: He is involved today, here, as we have faith to believe in His power. This should be required reading for every prospective missionary (both Latter-day Saints and otherwise!) and mission presidents."

—LORIANNE UPDIKE TOLER

(Founding president of ConSource.org, J.D. BYU Law, masters in history at University of Oxford, PhD studies in history at University of Pennsylvania, President Libertas Constitutional Consulting, served mission in Sydney, Australia.)

"I have spent over seven years as a missionary serving among the Polynesian people in the South Pacific who are extremely sensitive to the workings of the Spirit and are thus blessed with an abundance of the gifts of the Spirit. They are unlike many of the members of this day who live in a state of spiritual malnourishment because they do not discover and develop their spiritual gifts. Because the Polynesians seek after these spiritual gifts, they are richly rewarded.

"I believe that *Mine Angels Round About You* is a penetrating analysis of the remarkable ways the gifts of the Spirit operate among the missionaries of the Church. It clearly demonstrates that these gifts are present in modern times just as they were in the early Church. I believe reading about these experiences will encourage missionaries to step forward and claim their rich spiritual heritage. If missionaries will seek diligently after these gifts, they will not be hindered from enjoying blessings of a similar nature. Enjoying these experiences will serve to impart the quality of godliness to missionaries thus changing them for the better and making them more effective missionaries."

—DOUGLAS W. BANKS

(JD, CPA, partner at Deloitte & Touche, a leading corporate tax expert in the USA before retiring; Washington DC Temple presidency; former president of Tonga Nuku'alofa Mission, patriarch.)

"What a treat to read these respectfully documented examples. As they illustrated the diverse, subtle and tender ways in which the spirit can influence and intrude into our experience, I was glad to ponder anew the mystery and miracle of God's manifestations of His love."

—DAVID K. SANDBERG

(FSA, MAAA, CERA, senior consultant, Charles River Associates; president elect, president and past president of the American Academy of Actuaries; Society of Actuaries board member; International Actuarial Association Executive Committee, retired corporate actuary, Allianz)

"While I am not of the Christian faith, yet I believe that the Almighty works with men and women and helps them to the degree that they seek and are open to His help. This book documents many instances in which He has helped people who are laboring in His service to assist others to lift their sights."

—KABIR DUTTA

(Finance professor, Johns Hopkins University, former lecturer at Princeton University; lead economist at Boston Federal Reserve Bank, leading world authority on bank operational risk measurement, Hindu.)

"This is a wonderful, inspiring, spirit-filled book. I have been blessed as I read it.

"When I was a graduate student, Professor Babbel was my dissertation advisor at the University of Pennsylvania. As a scholar, Professor Babbel taught me to think critically and to challenge unsupported assertions by comparing them to well-established theory and to subject them to careful empirical testing. This book, however, presents a series of anecdotes that are in the realm of faith. They are not verifiable through traditional scientific methods of testing, measurement, or other empirical investigation. Yet each anecdote presents the possibility that God is actively involved in our lives. This book represents an invitation to believe that the gifts of the Spirit are real and are available to us today.

"So, what is the theory against which these stories may be compared? It is the scriptures. As I read each anecdote I think about the teachings and stories in the scriptures to see if the anecdote fits the patterns that have been revealed. Can we test these stories? Not in the traditional sense. But, we can ask God to teach us through the experiences of others. We have been told by Moroni that, 'by the power of the Holy Ghost ye may know the truth of all things.' Ultimately, stories of faith and the gifts of the Spirit are a blessing to those who experience them. They come as a result of faith rather than to create faith. Still, for the reader, these stories are invitations to believe and to experience faith and the gifts of the Spirit for ourselves.

"*Mine Angels Round About You* is a treasure trove of evidence that God still works by faith, that angels still minister to women and men, and that we have access to the gifts of the Spirit. But rather than simply accepting the anecdotes in this book as some kind of 'proof,' look at them as a series of testimonies that each of these people has experienced God's love. And, let that be an invitation for you to also draw near to Jesus Christ and receive these wonderful gifts in your life."

—CRAIG B. MERRILL

(Author, professor at Marriott School of Management, Brigham Young University; former MBA program director, PhD from The Wharton School of the University of Pennsylvania.)

"I was privileged to serve as president in the Oklahoma–Oklahoma City Mission. Your book brought back tender memories. I would like to share my witness that spiritual gifts and enlightenment were also evident in our mission and in the lives of missionaries. I have experienced many examples in the three years I served guiding missionaries. I have witnessed missionaries using their callings and priesthood to heal the sick, teaching with spiritual gifts and power, following promptings to miraculous effects and other manifestations of spiritual power. I have been prompted to say and do things interacting with missionaries that have edified and taught us from heaven. The fruits of the Spirit were often evident in our mission."

—JAMES R. ENGEBRETSEN

(Retired, Goldman Sachs; board of directors, Farmer Mac; entrepreneur; former asst. dean at BYU's Marriott School of Management and Director of Placement; former mission president, current YSA stake president in Provo, Utah.)

MINE *Angels* ROUND ABOUT YOU

MINE Angels ROUND ABOUT YOU

MIRACULOUS ACCOUNTS OF THE LORD'S HAND IN THE MISSION FIELD

DAVID FREDERICK BABBEL

CFI
An imprint of Cedar Fort, Inc.
Springville, Utah

© 2018 David Frederick Babbel
All rights reserved.

No part of this book may be reproduced in any form whatsoever, whether by graphic, visual, electronic, film, microfilm, tape recording, or any other means, without prior written permission of the publisher, except in the case of brief passages embodied in critical reviews and articles.

This is not an official publication of The Church of Jesus Christ of Latter-day Saints. The opinions and views expressed herein belong solely to the author and do not necessarily represent the opinions or views of Cedar Fort, Inc. Permission for the use of sources, graphics, and photos is also solely the responsibility of the author.

ISBN 13: 978-1-4621-2217-2

Published by CFI, an imprint of Cedar Fort, Inc.
2373 W. 700 S., Springville, UT 84663
Distributed by Cedar Fort, Inc., www.cedarfort.com

LIBRARY OF CONGRESS CATALOGING-IN-PUBLICATION DATA

Names: Babbel, David F., 1949- compiler.
Title: Mine angels round about you : miraculous accounts of the Lord's hand in the mission field / compiled by David Frederick Babbel.
Description: Springville, Utah : CFI, an imprint of Cedar Fort, Inc., [2018] | Includes bibliographical references.
Identifiers: LCCN 2018007691 (print) | LCCN 2018012041 (ebook) | ISBN 9781462129270 (epub, pdf, mobi) | ISBN 9781462122172 (perfect bound : alk. paper)
Subjects: LCSH: Mormon missionaries. | Christian life--Mormon authors. | Church of Jesus Christ of Latter-day Saints--Doctrines. | Mormon Church--Doctrines.
Classification: LCC BX8661 (ebook) | LCC BX8661 .A54 2018 (print) | DDC 266/.9332--dc23
LC record available at https://lccn.loc.gov/2018007691

Cover design by Shawnda T. Craig
Cover design © 2018 Cedar Fort, Inc.
Edited and typeset by Elise Babbel Hahl and Nicole Terry

Printed in the United States of America

10 9 8 7 6 5 4 3 2 1

Printed on acid-free paper

We dedicate this book to the Savior of the World and to His Heavenly Hosts, without whose matchless power and support there would have been nothing to write.

We also dedicate it to the missionaries, whose faith, humility, dedication, and selfless sacrifice summoned the powers of Heaven to bless the lives of countless others.

CONTENTS

Foreword

Then all the multitude kept silence, and gave audience to Barnabas and Paul, declaring what miracles and wonders God had wrought among the Gentiles by them.

Acts 15:12

Are the gifts of the Spirit, so well attested in scripture, still available to us today? This book is a testimony from a small sampling of missionaries of Jesus Christ, who served together in one small part of the world, that God still blesses the lives of His children through the gifts of the Spirit.

The missionary accounts shared in this volume are all eyewitness recitals. Almost all were recorded contemporaneously or within a few days of when the underlying events occurred and were recorded by those who witnessed what transpired. Many were corroborated by multiple witnesses. The materials used to compile these stories are what historians refer to as "primary sources"—original documents and objects, which were created at the time under study. These "are the raw materials of history" that are so coveted by serious chroniclers. Such missionary experiences are among the most recited stories in the sacred scriptures, and they are meant to be shared. What would the New Testament be without the stirring missionary accounts of John the Baptist, Barnabas, Silas, and Paul? And who cannot be inspired by the danger-fraught missions of Amulek, Alma, and the four sons of Mosiah that are recounted in the Book of Mormon?

The eyewitnesses who recorded the experiences recounted in our book were young women and men who were called to serve full-time missions in the Church of Jesus Christ of Latter-day Saints (sometimes referred to as LDS or Mormons). They were between the ages of nineteen to twenty-seven. I know well each of these individuals and have no doubts regarding the truthfulness of their accounts. Nonetheless, I personally verified many of these accounts through interviews and corroborating witnesses. The accounts herein were recorded in their personal journals, in letters to the mission president as a part of their weekly activity reports, and in personal interviews when they had no idea that they would ultimately be shared. During the course of their missions, the accounts related in this book were generally not shared. On occasion, however, I would relate select stories with groups of missionaries, although I never revealed the identities of those involved nor the locations where the events occurred. (I did this to guard against any natural tendency that some people might have to seek personal recognition.) However, before submitting the manuscript of this book to publishers, I did receive each missionary's kind permission to include their name and stories in this volume.

I have lived long enough to see that marvelous spiritual gifts are sprinkled among people of many faiths, and even among those who have no religious beliefs. The gifts of God are not restricted to Baptists. Or Catholics. Or Jews, Mormons, Muslims, and Hindus. No organization has a corner or monopoly on the gifts that God grants to His children. The Light of Christ is available to all—Christians and non-Christians, and yes, to atheists.

Although this book focuses on gifts that the LDS missionaries experienced, witnessed through LDS lenses and expressed in LDS parlance, I celebrate all experiences that lead us closer to God and give us greater compassion for others. As the Apostle Paul wrote, we all "see through a glass, darkly," through different prisms and filters. Yet by sharing our experiences with others, we can obtain a clearer view of the Lord's works and dealings with humankind. Each gift is precious. Many are sacred. All are designed to uplift and to edify.

We share in this book a treasure trove of accounts—not in the spirit of boasting, but of rejoicing in the glory of the Lord (Alma 26) and in His active role in the work of missionaries. Our hope in recounting and exchanging these precious accounts is that readers will be edified. We did not compile these accounts for any personal gain. Any and all royalties will go to charity and the support of future missionaries.

Acknowledgments

Behold, there shall be a record kept among you.

D&C 21:1

As a university professor whose career has been dedicated to economics research, but whose avocation has been in studies of religious history, I could not resist compiling the accounts recorded in this book. Throughout my life I have benefited from others who freely shared their life experiences and gifts from God and I have felt impelled to share what is contained in this book. My wife, Mary Jane Babbel, was an ideal missionary companion to assist in presiding over the Brasília Mission, and played an essential role in every aspect of that mission. If John the Baptist or Paul had a missionary companion like her, their missions would have gone a lot better!

I thank Prof. Oliver Hahl whose cogent observations at the outset and unremitting encouragement throughout the project impelled me to undertake the task. I received editing help and great ideas from Dr. John and Karisa McAllister, Tara and Prof. Evan Haglund, and most of all Elise Hahl, whose vision and guidance were indispensable. Our youngest child, Tyson, agreed to sacrifice his last three years of high school at a top Pennsylvania school in response to our mission call and face the unknown educational opportunities available in Brasília.

The 505 missionaries who served with us were, of course, the inspiration for the book. Their dedication and faith went far beyond what I had expected, and I will feel eternally grateful for the privilege of serving with them. The sometimes seen, more often unseen but felt presence of spirit beings and the Savior were what kept them safe, reinforced their resolve to labor diligently, and sanctified their toil. Missionaries were comforted to know that they were not alone.

I also am indebted to the reviewers who saw earlier versions of this volume. They include Frances "Butch" Cash, Lorianne Updike Toler, Prof. Craig B.

and Andrea Merrill, Douglas W. Banks, Colonel Frank Petty, Joyce Woolf, David K. Sandberg, Profs. Laurel and Gael Ulrich, Pres. James R. Engebretsen, Prof. James McDonald, Prof. Noel Reynolds, Prof. Kabir Dutta, Prof. Richard Bushman, Dr. RoseAnn Benson, Prof. Eric Huntsman, Andrew Ehat, Jon Jensen and Joanne Smith. I cannot detail here the many ways in which these wonderful men and women encouraged my efforts and offered incredible assistance. One of them, a retired CEO of two Fortune 500 companies, actually performed meticulous copy editing on the entire book and enthusiastically offered several suggestions for the presentation. Another called and wrote me several times with detailed feedback on many of the experiences related in this volume and how to interpret them. Four, who had also presided over missions, provided excellent judgment and reassuring corroborating witnesses of the active role of heavenly hosts in their missions.

I also thank Antonio Maiquel Nunes and Bladimir Garcia for their superb Portuguese and Spanish translations of this book, which are also scheduled for release in 2018. The skilled editorial team at Cedar Fort was also very helpful in producing the English language volume.

Above all, I acknowledge He who is above all, Jesus the Anointed One, whose active role in the missionary work was astonishing and wondrous to me. I did not anticipate and would not have believed it had I not witnessed it time and time again.

Chapter 1

INTRODUCTION

But seek ye first the Kingdom of God and his righteousness; and all these things shall be added unto you.

Matthew 6:33

It started with a ringing phone one November afternoon in 2001. My wife, Mary Jane, was the one who picked it up.

"Hello?"

"Hi," answered the voice on the other end. "This is Dallin Oaks."

She paused for a moment. What were the odds, she wondered, that the person on the other end of the line was actually Elder Dallin H. Oaks? From the Quorum of the Twelve Apostles? Standing in the kitchen of our home in suburban Philadelphia, she thought that scenario seemed unlikely. My wife strained to read the caller ID, but she wasn't wearing her glasses and the glare from the sun made it hard to read the print.

"Could I speak with your husband?" said the voice.

"He's not here right now," she said warily, "but the class he teaches is over and he should be home soon."

The caller said he'd try again at 5:30.

"Dave, someone who says they're Dallin Oaks wants to talk to you at 5:30," Mary Jane told me over the phone. I was sitting in my office at The Wharton School of the University of Pennsylvania, going over a few things after teaching a class. She reminded me that only a couple of months earlier, I had left a phony message for Burke at his law office. (I had told the receptionist, "Tell Burke that [President] Boyd K. Packer was calling and that he'll call again later." I was just having a little fun . . . I figured that Burke, who was known for his heterodox doctrinal views, would quickly assume it was a prank and laugh, albeit nervously.) Mary Jane thought that maybe Burke was paying us back.

"It *does* sound a lot like Elder Oaks, though," she said.

I looked at my watch and saw that 5:30 was less than half an hour away. Just in case the caller really was Elder Dallin H. Oaks of the Quorum of the Twelve, I hurriedly left for home.

The phone rang right after I walked through the front door. From the minute I heard the distinctive voice on the other end, I could tell that this was not a prank phone call at all. The voice was unmistakably the one I had heard speaking in general conference so many times. After exchanging some niceties with the *real* Elder Oaks, I listened as he got down to business. He indicated that he wanted to explore with me and my wife a possible calling that would involve full-time, intense service for a period as long as three years. He asked if it would be convenient for us to meet with him during his next trip to the East Coast in early January. I gulped out a "yes." He said that we should be prepared to consider and discuss with him all of the ramifications of such an interruption in our careers and any other impediments that would hinder us from accepting such a calling at this time.

When Mary Jane returned from her engagement, she asked if "Elder Oaks" had actually called, and I reported back what had happened.

Mary Jane and I drove to the appointed location for the interview in early January and arrived about forty minutes early. We parked a few blocks away, where we could have some seclusion and discuss the possible calling.

Together we reviewed the many impediments to accepting an assignment of this magnitude at this time. After enumerating and discussing them, we both bowed our heads in the car and began to pray about it. In my prayer, as I began to recite the various considerations, I seemed to hear the bewildered voice of my recently deceased father, saying, "My son, haven't you learned anything from me?!" Then appeared in my mind a half sheet of paper with eight names written on it. His was listed at the bottom.

More than fifty years earlier, my father had seen that same piece of paper with the handwritten names on it. He came upon it while he was organizing documents in the European mission headquarters for The Church of Jesus Christ of Latter-day Saints, in London. My father, thirty years old at the time, was serving a special humanitarian mission with Elder Ezra Taft Benson. The year was 1946, just months after the end of World War II.

My father asked Elder Benson where to file the piece of paper with the list of names and wondered aloud why his own name was included on it. He recognized most of the other names—well-known men with various European ties.

According to my father's recollection, which he related to me when I was a young man and recorded in his personal history, Elder Benson remarked, in essence, "Well, I guess I can tell you about it now. When I was asked to preside over the European missions after the war, I was told to call a missionary companion to assist me in getting urgent relief supplies to the troubled people in Europe. I needed someone who would be ready to leave at once due to the desperate situation of the people of Europe and be willing to stay for a long but indefinite period. I contacted several of the prior mission presidents and asked them whom they would recommend. You were on everybody's list, but they also recommended some more prominent, established men." (The mission presidents knew my father from his first mission in Germany, where he had served as mission secretary in all four of the German-speaking missions right before the war began.)

Elder Benson went on. "I was familiar with the other people but knew nothing about you, so I placed your name at the bottom of the list. As I called each of the others, they were not in conditions that would allow them to accept such a calling. Each of them had other impediments to service at that time, such as being involved in a research program, having professional duties, starting a business, experiencing temporary financial limitations, having educational aspirations, caring for a young family, and so forth. I finally reached your name, and when I called you on New Year's Eve [of 1945], there was no hesitation in your willingness to serve. I later learned that you had several of those same impediments to service, yet you and your wife did not let them get in the way."

My parents' decision to have my father serve a mission with Elder Benson for what turned out to be sixteen months seemed like an overwhelming sacrifice at first, but it became a huge blessing from the Lord. Leaving his wife and newborn daughter in the care of his parents-in-law, my father was able to bless many Europeans as well as his own family for generations to come. Additionally, many were benefitted who read my father's published accounts of the extraordinary faith exhibited by the struggling Europeans after the war.[1]

I got the message.

After we finished our prayers, individually and together, I told my wife of the image that came to my mind and what I seemed to hear. I discussed with her the message that was coming through to me loud and clear. She, too, had felt that any impediments we might have at that time toward serving a mission paled in comparison to the importance of accepting a calling to serve the Lord, being willing to sacrifice whatever was necessary, and trusting in the Lord's timing. We

1 See Frederick W. Babbel, *On Wings of Faith* (Bookcraft, 1972). Elder Benson later served for eight years as Secretary of Agriculture under President Eisenhower.

decided to go to our interview and, if asked, tell Elder Oaks that there were no important barriers to preclude our service.

After about an hour of discussion with Elder Oaks, he told us he would recommend us to preside over one of our church's missions. Because of our familiarity with the Portuguese language, he indicated that if we did receive an official calling, it would probably be to serve in a Portuguese-speaking country. A few weeks later, we received an official call from the First Presidency—we were to preside over the Brazil Brasília Mission starting on July 1.

Fast forward forty-one months later as our mission concluded and I sent the final report of our mission to President Boyd K. Packer. (The *real* President Packer this time.) Below is an excerpt of what I wrote:

> We have found that as missionaries gain experience with [teaching by the] Spirit, they are often able to receive other gifts of the Spirit as well. *I am not aware of any miracle, gift of the Spirit, or type of vision that was manifest since the First Vision up through the Nauvoo period that has not been manifest here among the missionaries.* . . . I have often felt as if standing on holy ground as I ponder their sacred experiences.

There was no hyperbole in what I wrote to President Packer. I am beyond grateful for my parents' example, which encouraged us to trust in the Lord and accept this assignment and led us to witness the Lord's hand among His missionaries.

The Lord promised His missionaries, "I have given my heavenly hosts and mine angels charge concerning you. . . . And whoso receiveth you, there I will be also, for I will go before your face. I will be on your right hand and on your left, and my Spirit shall be in your hearts, and mine angels round about you, to bear you up" (D&C 84:42, 88). We found that promise to be literally true. I often felt overjoyed as I watched what His missionaries accomplished through their faith in God. Truly, the Lord and His angels were enlisted and engaged in that work, and they surrounded His servants who labored to proclaim the gospel of Jesus Christ to those who thirsted for saving truths.

The following report of Sister Patrocínio was received when she was working with Sister Conceição in Sinop, Mato Grosso. It is one of many examples we witnessed of the literal fulfillment of the Lord's promise to missionaries.

"This week was very interesting. We were teaching an elegant and highly educated woman named Zilamar [who was undertaking post-graduate studies in the sciences]. We went and gave her the introductory lesson and explained about the happiness we feel for being members of the Church. She asked us if this was because we had received a response to our prayers about the veracity of the Book of Mormon. We responded affirmatively. She then made a very interesting observation that we had in our countenance a joy, peace and love. She accepted our invitation to read the Book of Mormon.

"She seemed to be a very cold woman, but her questions and observation said something better about her.

"A few days later we returned on a follow-up visit. We stayed there for over an hour conversing with her about her family, her husband, and her trials. She told us some things that she said she had never recounted to anybody, not even within her extended family, but said she told us because she felt a security and peace in us and felt she could confide in us.

"We thanked her and I offered to give a closing prayer. When I finished she looked at us with unwavering eyes and asked us if she could make a comment. We responded in the affirmative.

"Then she said: 'The first time you visited me I saw something different in you. I don't know whether you believe in angels, but I saw two angels on each side of you, but I was unable to see the faces of those beings because they had a brilliance emanating from their faces that was so strong. I know that you are protected by angels, because I saw those beings.'

"President, the Spirit touched us very strongly and we testified to her that they were with us because of the message which we imparted to her. We thanked her for sharing her sacred experience with us, and then she said: 'Before relating this experience to you, I first asked God if I should be telling you this. He said "yes." Therefore, I related it to you.'"

I have felt impressed to share a small portion of these stories—not because the Brasília Mission was an extraordinary place, or because the missionaries who served there were better than others, but because I think we need these stories (and I happen to have them as recorded contemporaneously by the missionaries). The scriptures and early records of the Church serenade us with miracles and wonders, which we preach from the pulpit and discuss in our classes. But if we don't communicate what's happening today as well, we may question, as Mormon warned we might, whether the day of miracles has ceased. "Or have angels ceased to appear unto the children of men? Or has he withheld the power of the Holy Ghost from them?" Mormon added, "Behold I say unto you, Nay" (Moroni 7:36–37). These heavenly manifestations are happening among us today, very often in the lives of full-time missionaries. In sharing some of their stories, I am encouraged by the prophet Isaiah, who wrote unto us: "And in that day shall ye say, Praise the Lord, call upon his name, *declare his doings among the people*, make mention that his name is exalted" (Isaiah 12:4; 2 Nephi 22:4; emphasis added).[2]

---

2 Of course there are those rare exceptions when we are impressed to keep certain sacred and personal experiences to ourselves. But imagine if the writers of the holy writ had kept heaven's acts secret—we would have no scriptures! (Well, perhaps the Song of Solomon and a few of the Leviticus chapters.)

While we were presiding over the Brasília Mission, the missionaries' experiences impressed me so much that I began making careful records of them. Some years after the mission, I asked Elise Babbel Hahl, a professional editor (and my daughter), to help select some of the written accounts to include in this volume, with permission from the missionaries.[3] We have woven them together thematically with a narrative to provide proper context.

We submit these witnesses humbly in hopes that faith in Jesus Christ and His teachings will increase. We hope that your appreciation for the active role of the Savior will grow—as ours has—as you read about His angels partnering with us in our attempts to spread the good news of the gospel.

3 These experiences, and many others, are included in *The Small Plates of the Brasília Mission*, a volume for private viewing in the LDS Church History Library.

Chapter 2
CONVERSION

When thou art converted, strengthen thy brethren.

Luke 22:32

For the tenth time in ten days, I was on my knees, praying for the same thing: to know if the Book of Mormon was true. I asked, just as I had nine times before, "Is it an authentic record of ancient scripture, or is it not?" I thought that the Lord would have rushed to answer a missionary's prayer, but there I was in mid-summer, fighting off mosquitoes in my sweltering, tiny, non-air-conditioned Rio de Janeiro apartment, learning the uncomfortable lesson of patience.

Just five months earlier, a sacred experience had taught me the reality of God and His infinite power. That made it all the more frustrating. Knowing that God lives, I couldn't help but wonder—why would He withhold an answer to my prayers?

It was 1970 and I was twenty years old. I had been serving a mission in Brazil for over a year. My district leader in Rio de Janeiro had set a goal for us to re-read the Book of Mormon during the months of January, February, and March, and I finished early, in mid-February. He had also challenged us to gain a witness from the Holy Ghost of the book's truthfulness by the end of March, so that we could all bear our testimonies to each other at the Easter meeting. I embraced this opportunity because I never felt completely comfortable testifying that I knew the Book of Mormon was true—in fact, I didn't know for sure that it was, although I had always felt it was true, never seriously doubting.

I went to bed on Day 10 without anything to report. Over subsequent attempts, my prayers grew longer. Still, by Day 20, I had not received an answer, but I kept on trying. Day 30 snuck up on me. *Nada*. Nothing! I felt treated as if I were making a phone call to heaven every time I prayed: "Is that Elder Babbel calling up here again? Well, put him on hold." The exercise had become routine. I would brush my teeth, kneel down, ask, wait for a little bit, and then hit the pillow once again, unenlightened and increasingly bewildered.

As March drew to a close, I found, to my dismay, that the other district members had already received responses to their prayers. The only straggler was me.

I decided to start expressing my testimony to investigators more carefully. I would testify that I *believed* the Book of Mormon to be an authentic record of ancient peoples, but I wouldn't say anymore that I *knew* it was true. It made me feel less conflicted to be fully honest, yet I wished to bear testimony with the greater depth and conviction that knowledge brings.

Before Easter arrived, my mission president transferred me to another district, relieving the external pressure that I felt. Still, my quest continued, and still, nothing happened. It was somewhere around Day 40 when I had a key insight. Moroni, in the final chapter of the Book of Mormon, listed six qualifications for obtaining knowledge of the truth: *reading* the book, *pondering* upon the things read, *asking* the Father in the name of Jesus Christ if those things are true, asking with a *sincere heart*, asking with *real intent*, and *having faith in Christ*. (Interestingly enough, he didn't include worthiness on the list.[4]) When I thought about it, I recognized, for the first time, that I lacked *real intent*. My desire for a testimony had been for external reasons—to meet a district goal, and to be more convincing as I shared it with people interested in learning about our church.

But after so many failed attempts, I reached the point where I needed to know *for myself*. This desire grew quite intense over the following week.

On the forty-fifth consecutive night of my pleadings, I began my petition and felt something different—a jump in my heart—something that told me my prayer might not end with the usual "hold button" music this night. I began praying with more confidence and faith. I started my prayer by saying, with accumulated frustration (and immature impertinence), "Lord, tonight I'm not fooling around. I want You to keep Your promise, as I have done my part . . . I just need to know what *is* true by the power of the Holy Ghost as You promised." I paused and then rephrased the question: "Is the Book of Mormon what Joseph Smith alleged it to be: a translation through divine power of a record of

4 This was another key realization that dawned on me. Sometimes a person feels unworthy to get answers to prayers, and this feeling of unworthiness short-circuits one's faith that an answer will be received, which in turn can doom the whole effort. While personal worthiness is necessary for many things, it isn't for this.

an ancient people who inhabited the Americas?" I paused again and took a deep breath. "And I ask this in the name of Thy Son, Jesus Christ . . ."[5]

From my journal written in 1970 I quote: "I had scarcely uttered these last words and begun intensely concentrating when a wonderful, sublime power entered into me. It entered suddenly—a rush; I felt it all over (particularly in my heart region) and I started pouring out my heart in thanks. It surged within me for less than a minute—[perhaps much less] although it seemed to keep going and going—and was a divine power that *never* could have been mistaken for anything [earthly]. As that power entered me, the utter frustration I was feeling from so many unanswered prayers vanished in a split second and I was quickly brought to tears because of the wonderfulness of God, for He had ratified the marvelous promise made through His servant Moroni, and now . . . I, too, know that the Book of Mormon is a true record." This verity was indelibly etched upon my soul.

With this answer, I knew that I wasn't just doing a good turn in Brazil; I was leading people to the restored gospel of Jesus Christ, to truths that would expand their vision and lift their souls. Years later, I shudder to think how different my life would have turned out had I abandoned my quest on Day 44.

Elder Babbel as a young missionary in the North Brazil Mission

5 My purpose in phrasing the question that way is that I felt it could be answered with a "yes" or "no"—there was simply no equivocation. If I had asked a broader question—"Is the book true?"—it might not garner a simple response. Perhaps the original writers of the book had embedded some assumptions about geography or other peoples that were not precisely corroborated or drew some inferences that were incomplete. It could be difficult to get a direct answer, I surmised, if I asked the wrong question. Therefore, I phrased the question in a way that could, at least in theory, elicit a simple answer.

Later, as mission president, I was often privy to the struggles some of our missionaries were going through as they worked on receiving a testimony of the truthfulness of the restored gospel. For the first time in my life I was grateful for the prolonged struggle that I had gone through more than three decades earlier to receive a testimony—an endeavor that gave me great empathy for these young missionaries.

This book explores the many ways that the Lord bares His arm to assist His missionaries. During my tenure as mission president in Brasília, from 2002 to 2005, I saw time and time again how the Lord actively participated and led the work. I kept copies of the missionaries' letters to me as a record of the Lord's dealings with His young and humble servants, and the shared witness is breathtaking to me. But before we examine the lengths the Lord is willing to go to move this work forward, I am sharing stories from a few missionaries about gaining a testimony—the spark that starts it all.

Testimony at Last!

Elder Liava'a was one of our most accomplished athletes prior to his mission, and afterward he went on to become a football coach at a prominent university. He had tried to gain a testimony for a very long time and would fast regularly and pray earnestly to obtain one. Despite his tremendous efforts, he had not yet received the kind of spiritual witness that he desired. We had a discussion one day when I advised him to bear true testimony. If he did not have a spiritual witness, then he should convey his beliefs as beliefs, and not as sure knowledge. I told him that if he was always truthful, the Holy Ghost could testify through him and that a sure knowledge would eventually come, but in the Lord's own due time. He felt better about pursuing this course.

It took a while, and it was a trial for me to continue to counsel him to follow this course, which ultimately would bear fruit. Elder Liava'a followed my counsel, and eventually, he found out for himself that his beliefs were true. His search for a deeper testimony was met shortly after my wife and I completed our missions and returned to the United States. He wrote me the following letter.

"President, I've been asking the Lord for about two and a half years to know if the Book of Mormon is true and if Joseph Smith was really a prophet of God.

"As I cry this very moment, I testify to you that I KNOW THAT JOSEPH SMITH WAS A PROPHET OF GOD! President, the Lord himself has manifested the truth unto me through his Holy Spirit! My prayers have been answered!!! It's what I've been waiting for, for such a long time. I can finally tell people that I know the gospel is true and that it was restored by a prophet of God.

"President, I want to thank you for all the great counsel that you have given me. I wish you'd been here to see me bear my testimony at the Brasília North Ward. It was a Fast Sunday and we had a testimony Sacrament Meeting, three days after you left Brasília. Thank you so much, President. I have a great love for you. You will always be in my heart!"

Gaining a Sure Witness

The next story comes from an elder who had recently learned that his parents would be divorcing after three decades of a temple marriage. This devastating news led to a period of soul searching for the elder as he tried to make sense of his life and his mission.

"Do you remember that zone conference you gave when you spoke about testimony?" he wrote. "You shared an experience from your mission about your spiritual confirmation about the Book of Mormon. Well, your experience sunk pretty deeply in my mind. I thought about it quite a bit because I had done the same thing—asked, asked, asked and got nothing.

"A few weeks ago I was praying and I had a lot on my mind, so I was discussing it all with God. There came a point in the prayer when it didn't just bounce off the ceiling but made it all the way to God. It was as if God had picked up the phone and said 'Hello.' I felt one of the strongest connections between God and me that I have ever felt!

"I started to ask questions about what I needed to do with several problems and concerns that I had and to my surprise, He responded clearly and immediately—something that has never happened to me before—immediate answers, that is. I went through my list of concerns and then had the desire to ask about the Book of Mormon. So I did. I don't have the words to explain what I felt in that moment. It was like a burning heat, mixed with feelings of love, happiness, euphoria, and thankfulness all in one, which rushed through my whole body. I've never felt that before. I know that the Book of Mormon is the word of God, not because my Church believes it but because God Himself told me. That is something that I can't deny! I love the Lord!"

A Testimony of Faith

Thus far, the experiences in this chapter occurred in moments of solitude. Elder Radik, in contrast, gained a stronger testimony in the midst of his everyday service as a missionary. He came to our mission on leave from the U.S. Coast Guard Academy and was one of several wrestling champions that we happened to have on the mission. He recounted his faith-building experience to me on a visit to our family after his mission. I asked him to share it in writing. The experience occurred when he had been on his mission about six months and was serving in an area called Porto Nacional with his senior companion, Elder Housley. He wrote the following:

"At this point of my mission I had read several books from the missionary library. This was the first time in my life that I was really studying and understanding the gospel. It just all made logical sense. Because of this, my testimony shifted to more of an intellectual base than a faith or spiritual base. I then would have quiet moments when I actually lacked much faith and doubted my whole testimony. I was using worldly logic to explain things. I was upset because this was not giving me peace and happiness. But because I had a great desire to know the truth, as said in Alma 32, I decided to choose not to waste my time doubting and use my faith to come to a resolution.

"Shortly after, the Lord provided me with an opportunity to use my faith and to put spiritual things over worldly ones. We went to teach a family and my allergies started to act up really bad, with a runny, stuffy nose and other miserable symptoms that made it impossible for me to teach effectively. Normally when this happens, I can take medicine and about thirty minutes later, my allergies might start to get better. Being away from our house and in the middle of a visit, that wasn't an option. I thought about just letting my senior companion teach the discussion and take care of things after. But I wanted to do my part as a missionary and use my talents to help this family. Then it occurred to me that I could use my faith, so right then I said a silent prayer in my heart, knowing that the allergies would go away. Almost instantly, the symptoms stopped and I was able to finish the discussion without difficulty.

Elder Radik studying the scriptures

"My faith and testimony were greatly strengthened that day. Since then, I have been more capable of sacrificing and changing in my mission and life to have many other spiritual and learning experiences. I can now relax in the quiet and still moments of my life with much gratitude for my Heavenly Father and my Savior, with the comfort that They know and understand me."

Of course, the missionaries didn't just see their own testimonies grow; they helped thousands of investigators and less-active members embrace the truth. One of the most compelling stories came from Sister Stevens, who had been working with a woman named Renata.

The Sweeter Fruits of the Spirit

"On Saturday, we decided to fast with a less-active member who desperately wanted to know if the Book of Mormon was true. Renata got baptized when she was about fifteen years old, and shortly thereafter left the Church. Renata ended up getting married and now, about ten years later, she is in an abusive marriage that causes her and her two children to suffer. Over the past two and a half weeks, she has felt the desire to go back to her parents' church, and we have been visiting her at her parents' house because her husband wouldn't allow us in his and Renata's house. We gave her a Book of Mormon to read, but her husband found it, ripped it up and threw it away. Immediately thereafter, he was stricken with a severe case of gout and had difficulty standing and walking. We gave her another book, which she hid in her child's nightstand drawer so that she could have access to it in moments of need. Her husband later discovered this book too, and destroyed it.

"We went [to her parents' house] on Saturday afternoon to start our fast with her. President, the prayer she offered was so sincere that we were all full of the Spirit, and hopeful that her simple request to know if the Book of Mormon was true would be answered. We ended up giving her *Our Heritage* to read also, because a lot of her doubts were centered on Joseph Smith and the Restoration, but we told her that she should read the Book of Mormon because that was her purpose for her fast. That day was one I will never forget.

"During our specific fast for Renata, I was literally spiritually edified. Sunday came and as we arrived in the Church, we saw Renata standing there waiting for us with one of her children. With tears in her eyes she told us that she received her answer and knew the Church is true. Subsequently, after a small round of hugs and tears, she relayed the following:

"When she arrived home on Saturday, once again her Book of Mormon was 'missing' so she went to the next best thing she had, *Our Heritage.* She decided she would not go to bed until she had read the entire book, which she did despite the evil eye she repeatedly got from her husband. That night she dreamed that she was at a place with all her family, and they were all crying because her grandma had died. (Renata's grandma had already died and her vicarious ordinance work had been done in the temple.) Everyone there was desperately trying to cope with the death, and Renata stood up and raised her arms and with eyes closed said repeatedly, 'In the name of Jesus Christ, if this Church is true, my grandma will arise, in the name of Jesus.' After saying this, her grandma arose and gave her a hug and told her it was the true Church. Then they went out of that place, walking with arms interlocked, and Renata kept saying, 'Grandma, the Church is true! The Church is true!' She woke up Sunday morning and knew she had received her answer. She told us this story and with tears in her eyes told us that she had come home to her true home.

"In coming to church today, she had to face the wrath of her husband. She and her child got dressed and ready for church. The husband was suspicious and asked where they were going. 'To church,' they answered. 'Which church?' he asked. When they responded that they were going to our Church, he became irate and forbade them from going. He began to lock all of the doors and windows to keep them as prisoners in the house, yet they hurried out through a door that hadn't yet been locked. He saw them and took off running after them, cursing them as they ran out the gate. He was unable to catch up with them because of the gout that he was suffering, and they made it safely to church . . .

"But this is not all, President. In the Sacrament meeting she bore her testimony and told her story. Afterward, another less-active woman with whom we had been working, Michele, went up to the pulpit and bore her testimony of the truthfulness of the Church . . . She told everyone that she had come back to her home as well.

"President, I cry again as I think of the Spirit there in that meeting. Joy filled our hearts to realize that [the change] hadn't been anything that we personally had done, but that we had been the instruments in the Lord's hands to bring two of his daughters back to the fold."

This story, although wonderful in so many ways, also makes one grieve for the many women and children who are kept from the truth because of perilous situations at home. Renata showed great courage in her actions. I'm sure that the Lord will find a way to reach all people in Renata's situation, whether in this life or the next, and He will be very understanding.

The final story is about a friend of mine who felt a prompting he couldn't explain or ignore.

Read the Book of Mormon

Dr. Paulo was a cardiologist who lived in our Brasília ward boundaries. He had studied medicine at three top universities in the United States and then returned to Brazil to practice, where the president of Brazil appointed him to a lofty position in the Brazilian government.

Dr. Paulo was living in a domestic partnership with an inactive female member of our Church, and they had one child between them. The missionaries met with and taught him the missionary discussions over a period of almost four years. On two occasions, he came to the mission home and I personally taught him some of our doctrines and gospel principles.

He was a Spiritist of the Alan Kardec branch, which attracts a lot of highly educated Brazilians. Rather than condemning Spiritism as being from the devil, in our conversations I affirmed that it contained a number of truths, including some that were not a part of our official doctrine, but that it lacked some of the essential saving doctrines.

Dr. Paulo became more active in attending our Church, but did not join it. There were problems in his domestic partnership, and although he was intellectually comfortable with our doctrines and practices, his feelings were insufficient to motivate him to change religions.

Then one night, while leaving work, he walked to the parking lot to get into his car. He said that he distinctly heard a voice tell him, "Read the Book of Mormon!" He looked around the parking lot, which by that hour was largely abandoned, and could see that there was no one else there. Yet he had heard that directive very clearly.

He thought that he should follow the directive and read the book. It didn't take him longer than a month after that to get his life in order so that he could be baptized. After his conversion, he became one of the most helpful and valiant members of our ward and stake!

Dr. Paulo wanted the rest of his family to be sealed to him, so when we left Brazil, he had already arranged for his daughter from his first marriage to be receiving the missionary discussions in Switzerland, where she resided with her husband. His other daughter was also baptized. At the time of our departure, he was helping the missionaries out whenever and however he could.

Testimonies come in many different ways. Some point to a foundational experience for their beliefs, a paradigm shift, or an experience that left them with a new understanding. (This chapter contains mostly these kinds of examples.) Others find that their convictions have come gradually, even imperceptibly, but the sum of all the insights and inspiration over time can amount to a bright, vibrant testimony. Still others simply seem to be born with a strong faith (while some close to them may pass through long stretches of doubt or depression—in fact, their awareness of the testimony of others may even accentuate the pain, discomfort, and grief of their own journeys). The Lord communicates in different ways to different people, and it's important to understand how He speaks to each one of us. The most important thing, no matter how our witness has come, is what we do with it.

Chapter 3

"BUT I AM SLOW OF SPEECH"

To another [is given] diverse kinds of tongues; to another the interpretation of tongues.

1 Corinthians 12:10

One of the first hurdles many of the missionaries stumbled into, no matter how sturdy their testimonies, was the practical problem of how to share their beliefs in Portuguese, or even just to communicate at all with strangers. Even after speaking directly with Jehovah, Moses still hesitated when he was asked to be God's voice to the Hebrews and to Pharaoh. "But I am slow of speech," he protested (Exodus 4:10).

Stories about the gift of tongues have always amazed me, in part because I've had so little experience with the gift myself. At the Missionary Training Center prior to my first mission, I studied Portuguese diligently and always strove to use correct grammar. I prided myself on memorizing some 206 conjugations of the most common Portuguese verbs, sure that each verb form I learned would brighten my prospects in the mission field. The surprise came when I actually arrived in the mission field. I earned a nickname from the Brazilians for the way I handled their beautiful language: "Elder Batata na Boca" (Elder Potato in the Mouth). Two months dragged on before I could understand the Brazilians at all, and it took even longer for them to understand me. Only later was I able to communicate with a modicum of proficiency, but I never quite shook the nickname.

Some thirty-two years later, I was a new mission president in Brazil, speaking at my second stake conference there. I was delivering a talk that I had prepared and polished beforehand, using all of the elegant linguistic forms and refined vocabulary that I could manage. As I looked into the congregation, I noticed rows and rows of blank stares. Afterward, a visitor approached me, introduced herself as a schoolteacher, and proceeded to tell me that my talk had been completely unintelligible in Portuguese. "You might as well have given it in English," she said. "At least that way, some of us could have understood."

I learned—once again—that I needed to be humbled before I could communicate effectively.

These experiences led me to empathize deeply with those missionaries who were struggling with the language and to feel especially grateful for the gift of tongues when the Lord grants it to His servants. The variations of this gift are many, as the following vignettes demonstrate.

Gift of Interpretation of Tongues

During our final week of the mission, Elder Hatch sent this story about something that had happened earlier in his mission. He wanted to share it with us before we left.

"Well, I was straight out of the MTC with extremely little or no understanding of the Portuguese language. I could barely say my name and where I was from and whatnot, let alone understand the responses. The best way to describe my first month in the field is one word—'lost.' As soon as I got in the mission field we started getting word of our next Mission Conference that would focus on faith, which was scheduled for just one or two weeks into my mission. It was to be the 'best conference ever!'—or so everyone said.

"I got super excited but at the same time really frustrated and sad due to the fact that I would not understand anything. I really wanted to be able to participate and at least understand what would be said in this conference. So from the day I heard about it, I started studying like crazy and prayed like Enos. I just prayed that I would be able to understand everything at the conference and be able to get out of the conference everything possible. I prayed and studied every day up until the day of the conference, but until that date nothing had changed.

"We were on the bus going to the conference and I was still lost. But the miracle happened when we got to the chapel. We got to the front door and as soon as I stepped through the doorway, it was like a switch had flipped. I understood everything as clearly as English! But I noticed that I still couldn't say hardly anything. Just understand.

"I went through the whole conference picking everything up. It's interesting because all of my notes from the conference are in English due to the fact that I didn't know how to write it all down in Portuguese. At the end of the conference when we were leaving the chapel, as soon as I stepped out through the doorway, it was like flipping another switch. I couldn't hardly understand or speak anything again. So basically it went back to normal. Until this day, to me, that was the best conference yet!"

Speaking with Boldness

"My companion and I were at this guy's house," Elder Cromar wrote in his weekly letter. "We were there talking and I was going to start teaching. I started to teach about our Heavenly Father and then [the guy] started asking a bunch of questions. As things progressed, he got to the point where he was trying to teach us his beliefs. He started pulling out a bunch of anti-Mormon papers he had gotten off the internet and started to tell us that if we didn't read the Bible and believe in Jesus Christ, we were going to hell. [I became quiet as] my companion, Elder Healey, did an awesome job at defending us against every way he attacked the Church. Elder Healey also tried many times to teach him, but he didn't get anywhere.

"The entire time [Elder Healey was defending our beliefs] I didn't say a word because I still cannot speak well and when conversations are going fast, it is very difficult for me to say stuff. The entire time, though, I could feel a burning feeling in my heart that kept growing and growing.

"The guy got to a point where he was prophesying to us and telling us Joseph Smith was not a prophet and a ton of other [garbage]. I was ready to explode, but not explode with anger—it was different. I wasn't mad or angry. I [had] feelings of peace, love and gratitude welling up within me and I wanted this guy to know the truth. Finally, Elder Healey decided we weren't getting anywhere and he bore his testimony with power. I had been praying in my heart throughout this time that I would have words given me to say, that I would be able to say them with power and that I would have the Spirit with me.

"After Elder Healey bore his testimony and we were about to leave, I asked if I could say something. As I started to speak, something really amazing started to happen. I began to speak and words just started coming to me, and I started to talk faster than I ever have before. I was able to conjugate verbs without trying. I don't remember everything I said, but I do remember that when I bore my testimony, I almost started crying. Through this experience my testimony was strengthened so much and a feeling of gratitude came over me more than any other time in my life. . . I became a living witness of D&C 100:5–6 and the promise in this scripture."

> 5 Therefore, verily I say unto you, lift up your voices unto this people; speak the thoughts that I shall put into your hearts, and you shall not be confounded before men;

6 For it shall be given you in the very hour, yea, in the very moment, what ye shall say.

"Keep Observing"

Elder Rebouças witnessed the fulfillment of this same promise during an experience with his companion, Elder Weishar—a brand-new arrival from North America. This companion was struggling immensely with the Portuguese language. The two were teaching a less-active member along with her parents, who did not belong to the Church, when the discussion took an unexpected turn.

"We had already taught several lessons to this family, but I sensed that they should hear the first lesson again, which they had heard innumerable times already. . . . My companion was assigned to teach the apostasy, so when his turn arrived to speak, the words simply wouldn't come out of his mouth. I felt the Spirit whisper to me: 'Keep observing.' I wanted to help him, but I also wanted to see his effort rewarded with the gratification of having succeeded.

"After attempting to speak for several minutes without success, he began to bear a testimony to them in broken Portuguese. He spoke about his difficulty in learning Portuguese, but said that one day he would succeed in speaking it. He spoke about the truthfulness of the Book of Mormon and the prophetic calling of Joseph Smith.

"The mother of the family looked toward me and said, 'Stop everything now. All of the questions I had about this gospel were just answered; all of the doubts that I had about this gospel have left. I know that this is the true church and that the things you are speaking are truthful.'

"I was shocked that a woman with so much knowledge about the Book of Mormon and the Bible, as she had, as well as so many firmly formed opinions, could have said such a thing! Although the testimony of my companion had been brief and spoken in a heavy American accent, that woman was able to be touched by the Spirit."

Gift of Tongues—Listening

We saw the gift of tongues working both ways—that is, helping foreign missionaries to understand and speak in a new tongue, but also assisting native-speaking missionaries to read, speak, and hear in a foreign language.

My wife and I were sitting in our ward's Relief Society room along with several others, waiting for the English broadcast of the 2003 October General Conference, when a Brazilian missionary of ours named Sister Prado walked in the room. I was surprised that she would be there, because as far as I knew, she spoke no English, but I said nothing to her. Most of the members and missionaries attended the broadcast in the chapel, which carried the simultaneous translation of the proceedings in Portuguese. After the first talk, I noticed that she quietly left the room. I assumed that she decided to attend the broadcast in her native tongue and thought nothing more of it. But a few minutes later, she returned and listened intently to the remainder of the session.

After the closing prayer, I asked Sister Prado why she decided to listen to the broadcast in English. She told me that she desperately wanted to hear and understand conference in its actual language, rather than hear it in words translated into Portuguese. She did not speak English, although she knew quite a few words. Still, she felt that if she could somehow hear the conference in English, she would be able to catch the meaning of the talks more accurately.

She had come to the conference broadcast in an attitude of fasting and prayer, petitioning for the gift of tongues so that she could benefit to the utmost from her conference attendance.

Sister Prado listened carefully to the first talk but struggled to understand it, as she explained in a letter that she wrote after the event. She had the capacity to understand as many as half of the words spoken, but they came in a random, unhelpful pattern. This was about the same that she was able to get without prayer and fasting, thanks to some rudimentary courses in English that she had taken prior to her mission.

Sister Prado retired to an adjacent room to pray. She explained, "I wanted with all my heart to understand, but could not. I prayed to the Lord that I knew He could help me understand everything that His servants were saying, and that I did not expect to leave that conference speaking English fluently; rather, I wanted only to comprehend and feel closer to Him by hearing directly the words spoken by His special witnesses."

She continued, "After praying to the Lord, I returned to hear the second speaker, Elder L. Tom Perry. It was [as] if the static had been taken from my ears and I could hear him with the same clarity that I could hear a person speaking in Portuguese. It was something I had never experienced before, and it was as if an enormous felicity became a part of me . . . I was so happy that I could join the words and phrases and within a few minutes, I understood everything that he was saying. It continued that way with each word of each talk for the rest of that afternoon, giving me such joy. I felt the Spirit so strongly. When I was able to hear the prophet [President Hinckley] speak, it was as if an immense joy took over me and I felt like exploding, and tears of gratitude ran down my face. Finally, I could experience the feeling of having such a special servant of God speak directly to us without translators and without pauses!"

She wrote that once her understanding was opened, she was able to comprehend even the subtler meanings and implications. It was an amazing experience for her and a testament to the way the Lord rewards the faith of His children. Even though it was not essential for Sister Prado to hear and understand the conference talks in their original language, the Lord was willing to grant her desire. I was impressed not only that she thought to ask for something out of the ordinary, but that she exercised her faith through fasting and prayer and then persisted until she received that blessing.

Gift of Tongues—Reading

This link between prayer, fasting, and the gift of tongues was something I noticed several times. I saw it once again in January of 2003, after I had just finished giving each missionary a Christmas gift—Elder John Groberg's book, *The Other Side of Heaven* (Deseret Book, 2001). I wanted the missionaries to learn from Elder Groberg's experiences in Tonga during his mission in the 1950s and hoped the book would lift their faith. Because the book was not available in Portuguese, I suggested to the missionaries that they use it for companionship study. The English-speaking missionaries could help non-English speaking companions to read and translate the book, which would be a good language exercise for both. I reminded the missionaries that Elder Russell M. Nelson of the Twelve had visited us in August and asked all missionaries to learn three languages during the course of their missions: Portuguese, English, and the Language of the Spirit.

Elder Russell M. Nelson and Dantzel Nelson, Walkyria Damiani and Area President Adhemar Damiani, President and Sister Babbel, Verla Sorensen and Elder David E. Sorensen on a mission tour of the Brazil–Brasília Mission

Elder Freire spoke some Spanish and knew a few Hebrew words (as well as his native tongue of Portuguese), but he had never studied English prior to his mission. He decided to make my challenge to read Elder Groberg's book a matter of fasting and prayer and requested that he be granted the gift of tongues so that he could benefit from the book and keep pace with the other missionaries. He was not asking the Lord for the gift of tongues in general, only for the ability to understand this one book.

Elder Freire told me privately, months later, that as he began to read the book, he was granted full comprehension. He could follow the text as if he were reading it in Portuguese. He said that the gift lasted until he reached the end of the book and that he was able to pick up on all of the fine details. His American companion witnessed the gift and marveled at Elder Freire's humble faith.

After reading the book, Elder Freire tried to read other things in English, but he said reading English now is just as if he were trying to read Chinese—that he has no recognition of words nor comprehension of phrases.

I can imagine how the Lord was pleased with the earnest desires of all these missionaries to feel closer to His message or to help other people to understand it better. I believe He wants the gospel message to be communicated with clarity and power, whether the message is intended for non-members, members, or even the missionaries themselves. How grateful I was to learn about these manifestations of the Lord's power.

Chapter 4

PROTECTION

May the God of Abraham, and the God of Isaac, and the God of Jacob, protect this people in righteousness, so long as they shall call on the name of their God for protection.

3 Nephi 4:30

The missionaries learned to rely on the Lord not only to gain stronger testimonies and to communicate them, but also to help them stay out of trouble. Although we did our best to teach safe practices to the missionaries, we hoped and prayed for their protection all the time. The Brasília Mission occupied an area equivalent to that of the Eastern Seaboard from Miami to Philadelphia and extending westward to the Mississippi River. It spanned two (and during some months of the year three) time zones and was overwhelming for me to consider the many ways something could go wrong in this huge, sprawling mission, especially when the nightly news blared horror stories about carjackings, shootings, and stabbings.

Some of the missionaries' letters told stories of times when their and our prayers were answered—when the Lord showed, through one way or another, that He knew how to protect His servants. Of course, each of these situations involved some near-disaster that could have ruined missions, or the missionaries themselves.

Sometimes protection came as a feeling; other times, as a warning; and still other times, as a physical force moving the victim toward safety. At times the protection was not even perceived until later.

The following vignette was recounted to me by Elder Fábio. His story, which I've translated as literally as I could, took place in the most humid city of our mission, where February temperatures hovered in the mid-nineties.

Moving Tables

"I learned a great lesson about how prayer can really be utilized daily in our life! This Tuesday, February 1, 2005, President Eduardo [the branch president] telephoned us asking for our help in moving to a new house. He was moving to a beautiful mansion located in the Serrano I Sector of Paraíso.

"We arrived at his house, and helped him load up the truck with all of his things, but we left for last a long table of solid marble that was extremely heavy to lift. At first glance, it appeared to be light, but as we attempted to lift it, our life forces were practically stripped from our bodies, it was so heavy! To lift it to the truck, it took five men: myself, my companion, President Eduardo, and two of the strongest men from our branch, Marlon and Sisley. With much sacrifice, we were able to move it. But the worst was yet to come, because the President's new house was very large and to attempt to lift this table again, after having already lifted it once, would be brutal and masochistic!

"When we arrived at the new house, we carried all of the furniture from the truck and placed it inside the house except for that table; finally, we had to deal with that table. We were exhausted, but we began to pick it up. Sincerely, I have never lifted anything so heavy in my life! When we couldn't stand to carry it any further, we stopped in the middle of the path and set it down to breathe a little. We were dead. That is when my companion [Elder Ries] had an idea and said, 'What do you think about us all offering a prayer and asking the Lord for help?' President Eduardo looked toward my companion and said, 'Let's do it!'

"Sisley was a bit incredulous at this and said, 'What will a prayer accomplish?' Then President Eduardo asked Sisley: 'Where is your faith?' Sisley pointed to his ample flexed biceps and responded, 'My faith is right here—in my arm.' I took advantage of this opportunity to tease him a little and said: 'Cursed is he that putteth his trust in the arm of flesh.' At that instant, Sisley got quiet and knelt down with us!

"In the prayer, my companion asked that the angels of the Lord might lift the table with us so that we could transport it safely without injuring ourselves. We arose from the prayer and began to pick up the table. Honestly, in my own hands that weight was not like it had been earlier. I could feel a difference, and at that moment I felt that President Eduardo and the rest must have borne the greater weight because I was hardly doing anything! We carried the marble slab the rest of the way to the house and placed it in the dining room on its iron stand. Afterward, the first comment was that of President Eduardo: 'Well, I don't know about you, but for me that table wasn't heavy like before!' My companion said the same thing. Marlon and Sisley were also surprised, and I began reflecting on how that table really did not weigh anything like it had before that prayer. One thing I know—the Lord is always disposed to help us when we really ask with faith, nothing doubting, whether it is to alleviate our heavy spiritual burdens of life, or to move a heavy table that I hope to never move again in my life!"

I spoke with Elder Ries about this experience a couple of weeks later. "What got in your mind that prompted you to solicit divine assistance in carrying a table?" I asked.

"Well," he answered, "we're promised as missionaries in D&C 84:88 that 'mine angels [shall be] round about you, to bear you up.' So I thought that if they were truly round about us, I might as well invite them to help instead of just watching!"

Such was the practical faith of these missionaries. I imagine that the angels were delighted to shoulder part of the heavy burden.

Any authentic collection of missionary stories would be incomplete without at least two vignettes about moving furniture, so I'll proceed to the next one.

At approximately two hundred seventy pounds and six feet, three inches, Elder Ware was a very strong and capable furniture-mover—but even he needed a miracle. Ten years later, he continues to ponder the experience.

A Gentle Push for a Gentle Giant

"When we arrived [at the new home], we began to unload immediately the heavy things. Although we had decided to unload the heavier items first, we had left an oven aside for quite some time and were already lifting some of the much lighter items up the flights of stairs. We were pretty exhausted from our labors but somebody had to do it, so I decided that I could take the six-burner oven by myself up the stairs to the new apartment. I knew that it wouldn't be too heavy for me to lift by myself. I started up the stairs and felt a little exhaustion, as I had already carried many things up to the apartment. I made it to the second flight and continued on to the third. It was on my way up the third flight that my testimony grew a lot. With an exhausted back and legs, and sweatier palms than a wet sponge, I made it about four steps and then suddenly lost my balance on the next step because the oven was getting very heavy in my arms and my body was tired; additionally, the tread depth of the stairs was quite shallow, which is no problem for the Brazilians, but for us large-footed Americans, it certainly can be a problem. [In a follow-up email and conversation confirming the details about this experience, Elder Ware told me he wore size 14 shoes, and that the shallow step treads could accommodate only about one-half to two-thirds of his foot, depending upon the uneven treads, and that the oven blocked his vision of the steps.] Suddenly, I lost my balance and started falling backwards. There was nothing I could do as I had already passed beyond the point of recovering my balance.

"It was then that a warm feeling rushed by me and through me and I, to my astonishment, felt a gentle push that saved my balance by falling forward—but only a little. I knew in this moment what had happened and that I had received some heavenly help. I will never forget this as long as I am living, and I wish I could tell that angel 'thank you.' I uttered those very words from my mouth quietly after this had happened and hope they were heard."

This experience showed two things to me. First, the servants of God do indeed have angels round about them—even in stairwells—and second, these angels are both attentive and quick! Elder Ware's mission would have come to an end that day, as he surely would have incurred grave injuries to his back had he fallen down several steep concrete stairs with an oven on top of him. The lessons from this experience stayed with Elder Ware as his mission unfolded.

The next example comes from two sister missionaries, Sister Lucas and Sister Ward, who both shared an experience they had on their way to teach a widow named Lúcia and her four children. My translated version of Sister Lucas's account tells most of the story, but Sister Ward's story adds detail as well.

Inspired Premonitions

Sister Lucas wrote, "We had been walking about five minutes to a scheduled discussion when [Sister Ward] told me: 'I feel that we shouldn't go there today.'

"I asked, 'Would you like to stop and think about it a little?' and [Sister Ward] replied in the affirmative.

"She asked me, 'What are you feeling?'

"I then remembered and related to Sister Ward that the same feeling had entered my heart earlier that day—the feeling that we should not go to this appointment—perhaps there was danger." [Sister Ward's account stated, "At the moment she said this, I felt the Spirit so strongly and it confirmed that we shouldn't go there. We didn't understand why, but we knew we couldn't go."] "It had come to me while I was in the home of a member writing a note, but I had dismissed the thought from my head, thinking I probably had it because it was rather chilly outside. Moreover, the investigator family was great, so why wouldn't we go there?

"Sister Ward then replied, 'I was also thinking this; after all, what other reason could there be? They are such a great family and are awaiting our arrival. But let's not go there! In the mouth of two or three witnesses shall every word be established.'

"We then returned in the direction of an outdoor telephone booth to call the family and reschedule. When we spoke with Lúcia to let her know that we would not be going there that night, and asked her to reschedule, I heard her children saying, 'Aww! Why aren't they coming? Everybody is here waiting! Do we have to wait until Friday? Is that the earliest they can come?' Even the sixteen-year-old, who wouldn't even smile at first when we had arrived for our first visit, was sad that we weren't able to go there that evening.

"Whew! It got me thinking, 'Why?' We were certain that we should not go there, but we wanted to know why not?"

Sister Lucas continued, "We didn't have to wait long to receive a response to our question. On Friday, we went to our rescheduled meeting with Lúcia's family . . . [They] had unfortunate news for us. They were about to leave . . . so our encounter would have to be rescheduled yet again.

"We sang a hymn with them, gave a prayer, and said our farewells. At that moment, Lúcia told us to be very careful if we were going to catch the bus, and that we should not linger long at the bus stop because it was very dangerous. She then said, 'They shot a young man this week here at the bus stop near our house. They tried to rob him and then shot him. This occurred last Monday. There were even police here afterward, but they were not able to catch the criminal.'

Sister Lucas (left) and Sister Ward (right) visiting a church member on the morning that they received a prompting to postpone an appointment that evening.

"I was shocked and asked, 'At what time did this happen?' Lúcia responded, 'It was at night, around 7:30 p.m.' Yikes! That was right about the time we would have been passing that location on Monday night en route to her home. I looked at my companion and her eyes were filled with tears, and I too began to shed tears because of the goodness of the Lord."

Many other missionaries saw in retrospect how they had been protected. The two accounts that follow, written by Elder Steele and Elder Diestler, were sent to me a number of months after the situations had occurred.

"The Road Less Traveled"

"In the month of April, 2003, lots of people in Cuiabá were very agitated because of the recently initiated war between the United States and Iraq. Elder Brown and I were working in that city of about 1.5 million inhabitants. One day we were headed to visit an inactive member. As we walked along the principal road, Elder Brown stopped, became pensive and said, 'Maybe it would be faster if we took another road to get there. I don't know why, but I am curious.' Therefore, we took 'the road less traveled,' and it wound up being approximately the same distance.

"The next week we were speaking with our zone leader, Elder Bernardes, and he asked us, 'What were you doing last week on Friday? Did you stay at home?'

"We responded, 'We worked like any other normal day. Why?'

"He replied, 'Didn't you hear? Last week there was an anti-American protest in the downtown section where you work and it got really violent.' We asked for more information from him and found out that the protest occurred at the same time and on the same road that we were walking along before taking our detour to 'the road less traveled.' Had we walked much farther along the principal road, we would have run right into the middle of the violent protest, and both being obviously American, we could have had some real trouble. I felt very protected by the Lord. I was glad that He was mindful of our perilous situation, helping two of His American missionaries avoid walking through the midst of this protest."

Because these elders didn't know about the danger they avoided until their meeting with the zone leader, almost a week later, it made me wonder how often the Lord protects us without our awareness. In this case, the inspiration came to Elder Brown in the form of a compelling curiosity—the desire to find a more efficient route. It was the kind of curiosity that might not have registered as a prompting, had the zone leader not informed the missionaries later on of the danger. Certainly, the Lord uses myriad ways to protect us, some of which we might never recognize.

Elder Diestler was tall and strong and posed an intimidating figure, even in a white short-sleeve shirt and tie. He might not have seemed like the type of person who needed much protection at all, but he perceived a warning from the Spirit about a situation more perilous than he realized.

Protection from Harm

"The situation began with a referral that Elder Young and I received from a member to visit a man and his family who had shown some interest in hearing the Gospel. This family lived in an outlying section of our area, without paved roads or streetlights. Unfortunately, because our schedule had been very busy, it took a few days before we were able to respond to the referral, but one evening, around nine p.m. or so, we found that we were passing the road that would have led to his house. We decided that we might as well stop by and try to set an appointment as our last task for the evening before heading home.

"We followed the road for about a hundred yards or thereabouts, and came to an extremely steep dip in the road that led into a very deep ravine. The road degenerated as it ran farther into the ravine until it was little more than a worn trail, maybe a foot or two wide, that crossed over a running creek and through a great deal of underbrush. The sides of the ravine were impossibly steep, and it seemed at best precarious to go into it in the dark of night. Elder Young and I stopped and counseled briefly with each other, trying to decide what to do. We both had a great desire to visit this family and to share the Gospel with them, and the idea of waiting another day didn't, at first, seem right. We discussed the matter, and decided that it really was too dangerous to go climbing down and up a steep ravine filled with rocks and brush at 9:00 at night with no light to work with.

"Instead, we considered going up a block, following a street that would help us avoid the ravine without any terribly serious detour. However, as we discussed this, the Spirit of the Lord began to whisper to me, and the eyes of my understanding were opened. I could see in my mind the images of three men, drunk, who were walking down that same stretch of road that we were considering taking. One of the men, I distinctly recall, was wearing a white T-shirt and another was carrying a knife, and the Spirit told me very clearly that if we were to take that road at that time, we would be assaulted by these men. I recounted the entire revelation to Elder Young, who unquestioningly accepted it.

"We turned back to the ravine, still greatly desiring to contact this family, and we decided that we would brave the ravine even in the dark. However, before we could take more than two steps we heard, both of us, very distinctly, a cruel, cold, evil laugh coming from the darkness deep within the ravine. The laugh made our blood run cold, especially because we could see no sign of any human life in the darkness.

"We turned around, shaken to the core and silently praying that the Lord would forgive us for not contacting the family on that night, and went back home. The next morning, in the light of day, when the danger was gone, we took the higher road, avoided the ravine and contacted the family, scheduling a teaching appointment with them for later that week.

"More than a week passed. Elder Young was transferred out of the area and I was assigned to train Elder Arruda. On his second or third night in the area, we had an appointment to make a follow-up visit with this family. The appointment was in the early evening hours, and we set out along the upper road, which had become our preferred path for arriving at this family's house. As we walked along the street, three men passed us, one of whom was wearing a white T-shirt. The men, completely sober, took no notice of us, but I stopped as they walked by. I recognized that these men were the same men that the Lord had shown to me on that night we had first wanted to visit the family. There was no danger this time, but it confirmed to me what I had been shown before."

I received a very brief but powerful note from Elder Rodrigo, who wrote about a night when he was able to witness heavenly help.

Night Protection

"The other night we were walking along a road that was very dark. There was no lighting that night. I was a little fearful. It was so dark that I could not even see my own feet! I told Elder Silva about my fear and he playfully responded: 'Aren't you seeing the battalion of angels surrounding us?' I replied, 'It is true, they are here to sustain us.' At that moment I saw someone dressed all in white passing by my side. Immediately, I looked behind and around us, but didn't see anyone else. I know that the angels are truly around us. I know that they are at our summons, ready to help us. I know."

Although the Lord often helps his servants avoid risky situations altogether, sometimes he helps his missionaries to face them. The following three accounts are examples of times that the missionaries received help as they encountered danger head-on. The first is from Elder Hatch.

Beware of Dog

"It all started on Sunday when we went with a member to teach the first lesson at the home of a member referral. When we got there, we clapped our hands in front of their gate [which is a Brazilian custom like knocking on doors], and she came and let us in. We entered into the yard and made our way toward the house, which was about ten meters away from the front gate. When we got to the house, or close to the house, we ran into her really large German Shepherd dog that was chained to a tree. Let me just tell you that he wasn't too happy to see us. The chain allowed him to be right where we were going to enter the house, so we had to walk around to the right and enter the house through the side service entrance—an area where she washes clothes and stuff—where we were out of reach and out of sight of the dog.

"The dog stopped barking, so we sat down and taught the lesson. Because I did not see or hear the dog during the lesson, I forgot about him completely. We taught the lesson, ended and got ready to leave. So I went first, and walked straight out of the front door without even thinking that I would have to take the side door to avoid the dog. As I walked out the front door, I found myself less than one meter from this dog that was lying on the ground to my right. [At this point, Elder Hatch asked me to refer to his diagram in the letter. The diagram illustrated the positions of the front gate, side door, front door, big dog, and chain.] The length of his chain allowed him a lot of leeway, as I said. His limit was about two meters beyond where I was standing. When I saw him, he saw me. I froze completely. He stood up, growled, and then jumped at me with his jaws wide open and aimed at my neck. I did not move at all, nor could I have moved, but at the last second, the 'Fourth Watch,' as it were, I was pulled quickly to my left about two and a half meters, just beyond the dog's reach. President, I had absolutely nothing to do with getting pulled out of the dog's reach, nor did my companion, who was directly behind me and watching the whole thing. That day I learned the reality of D&C 84:88. Someone was looking out for me. The first thing that I can really remember doing was saying a silent prayer of thanksgiving to God. I don't think that the dog would have killed me but he would have seriously injured me, that's for sure. This experience really had a big impact on me. That scripture really has meaning to me. I am so grateful for divine promises!"

I spoke with Elder Hatch's companion, Elder Raimundo a couple of weeks later while he was in attendance at a zone conference and he confirmed that he watched as his companion, without moving his legs, had been suddenly whisked away from the dog.

The next account was one that I have marveled about ever since Elder Ware recounted it to me in an interview on April 8, 2005. (Elder Ware was the missionary who struggled to lift an oven up the stairs, as recounted earlier in this chapter. Some missionaries have all the fun, I guess.) Separate follow-up interviews with him and his former companion clarified the details of the experience before I put it into writing, and then Elder Ware reviewed and supplemented this final account.

Airborne Unicycle

Elder Ware and Elder Hammond were riding their bicycles on the shoulder of a street that was bordered by a sidewalk and, immediately adjacent to the sidewalk, a row of short buildings. The shoulder was in need of repair, and so the elders would steer clear of road damage and merge into the regular lane of travel as occasion required.

One time when they swerved to avoid a damaged section of the road shoulder, a motorcyclist who was traveling at a high velocity (estimated by Elder Ware and the motorist at fifty miles per hour) was unable to avoid directly hitting the back of Elder Ware's bicycle. The impact was severe and crumpled the rear half of the bicycle while sending Elder Ware, a missionary about the size of a college linebacker, soaring into the air along with what remained of his bike. Elder Ware quickly reached the cruising altitude of his voyage. The motorcyclist swerved back and forth as he attempted to bring his vehicle under control.

"I was airborne for what seemed to me like a few seconds, and was sailing high enough that my line of vision was even with the rooftops of the nearby buildings. I traveled forward until my front wheel was about 3–4 feet above the head of my companion, Elder Hammond, who was riding his bicycle while receiving a call on his cell phone. A quick impression came to me that I should securely hold onto the handlebar. This impression was definitely more than just an instinctual reaction." As Elder Ware was looking down upon his companion's head, he said that he felt that his trajectory was being guided in slow motion, and that he was being held upright. He worried that if he came down upon Elder Hammond's head, his companion could be killed. He wrote, "I felt very panicked when I realized that I might actually land on my companion Elder Hammond, and it was also frustrating to me that he was just jabbering away on the phone [handling mission business] and didn't even know about the craziness that was soaring above and behind him. Yet it seemed to me as if I were a mute not being able to yell or shout or even talk at all as I was left speechless." Instead, he and what remained of his bicycle were guided to a very soft landing directly behind his companion. Elder Ware stated that the impact of his landing was about the same as the impact of being on your toes and then having your feet hit squarely upon the ground. His velocity slowed so that he simply landed on his feet and stood upright. By then his companion registered the noise, had stopped his bike, and was looking around to see what the commotion was all about.

"Upon landing on what had become my unicycle, I turned around and noticed that the rear of my bike had been decimated. The motorcyclist, after hitting my bike, was unable to regain control and crashed his vehicle within seconds. He flipped repeatedly on his motorcycle, skidded perhaps sixty feet, and crashed in front of my landing site, so I walked forward to greet him and see if he was okay, and of course to make a contact. The motorcyclist was injured and was very surprised that I was even alive and completely unhurt. He explained to me that he had been going as fast as his motorcycle could go because he was late for a university class. That was why he was unable to control his motorcycle enough to avoid hitting me when I swerved outward into the traffic lane. I gave him a pass-along card. The address he gave me turned out to be a false one, perhaps because the man was afraid of legal complications. My companion asked for a full explanation when he saw my destroyed bicycle!"

Elder Ware and Elder Hammond getting fingers bitten by large parrot.

Elder Hammond with bike; note at left the last known photo of the back wheel of Elder Ware's ill-fated bicycle.

This was an unusual style to make a "contact," to be sure, but knowing Elder Ware, not beyond one's imagination! In one of our conversations I remarked to Elder Ware that it was amazing he did not descend with greater force. Elder Ware shrugged his ample shoulders, saying that the laws of physics may not apply in the same way when there is angelic help.

Power of the Nametag

Two of our sister missionaries separately wrote the following accounts in their weekly reports. One night the sisters were passing through a lengthy underground walkway that stretched underneath three highways in Brasília when they were accosted by a thief. The thief grabbed Sister Ferreira by the hair and secured her while he robbed her. He then tried to rob her companion, Sister Lucas, while still securing Sister Ferreira by her long, thick black hair. Sister Lucas would have none of it and pointed to her missionary nametag. I should note that neither of these powerful sisters weighed much more than ninety pounds. The translated accounts are written below.

From Sister Ferreira: "We recently had the following experience: We customarily pass under the freeways by using the underground tunnels. One day, as we were crossing under the highways, a man approached us, grabbed onto my hair and said, "This is an assault. Give me everything you've got!" I gave him the only five reais [about $2.50] that I had with me. Sister Lucas didn't have any money, but the man kept on insisting, asking for a cellular phone, money, etc. I was very surprised when, within a fraction of a second, Sister Lucas said, 'I have nothing.' She even showed him the insides of her purse and again said, 'We have nothing. We are from the Church . . .' and began to show her missionary nametag. The man completely changed his physiognomy [facial appearance], let me loose, returned the money, and left rapidly.

"One more time, I saw how the Lord truly protects us and how His angels surround and sustain us."

From Sister Lucas: "Two people we contacted called us 'angels' on the same day. And this same day we were assaulted, or more accurately, almost assaulted. I will never forget the face of the thief when I showed him my missionary nametag and said, 'We are of The Church of Jesus Christ.' I didn't even have time to complete the phrase, because the thief let loose of Sister Ferreira at that very moment, returned the money to her, and said, 'Get lost! Go away from me and don't say anything about this to anybody!'

"What was interesting is that [as he glanced slightly above my head] his entire visage changed, he made a face that he couldn't do such a thing with us, and then he let Sister Ferreira loose.

"I have a strong testimony of the 'power of the nametag' as you might call it. But really, I know that angels surround us and sustain us (D&C 84:88), and that this is the Lord's work, and that He keeps watch over us."

The penultimate story is a missionary diary excerpt I received from Sister Wetzel, a civil engineering graduate and accomplished college athlete prior to her mission. If any missionary was prepared to handle a dangerous situation, she was, but on this occasion the threat was directed at her companion, not her.

A Shield of Light

"I had been serving in Taguatinga with Sister Monteiro for two transfers when I received the news that I'd be transferred to Cáceres [about 800 miles to the west of Taguatinga and near the border of Bolivia]. The next two days were busy as we tried to get things in good shape for Sister Monteiro, who would be training a new companion. Early Tuesday evening, we stopped by an ATM so I could withdraw money for my trip to Cáceres the next day. I tried both my mission credit card and my personal debit card. Neither would work. I remember thinking that it was odd, when a thought came very clearly to my mind: 'You will be robbed tonight.' I was taken back by the clarity, and even looked around. I kind of got scared, but remembered that President Babbel had been explaining to us that 'fear is below the line of demarcation that separates the territory of God and the territory of Satan,' so I brushed it aside, although I did try to be more careful about where we walked the rest of the evening.

Sister Wetzel, Dário, Déborah, Adriana, and Sister Monteiro

"We finished everything we needed to do and were headed home at about 9:30. We were in a great mood and were enjoying the final hours of our time together. As we walked in the door of our apartment, I went ahead and fumbled to turn on the light. I turned when Sister Monteiro, about five feet behind me, gasped, and I saw her struggling with someone in the doorway. There appeared to be another person with him. I went back to help. Sister Monteiro let her bag go and the robber took off. For a split second I thought of chasing him, but wisdom prevailed and I simply watched the robber run into the night as I slammed the door shut. I still have no idea where they came from. Sister Monteiro fell into my arms, half sobbing, telling me that EVERYTHING of importance was in the bag: her scriptures, her camera, her personal and mission bank cards, her identification, her money, the keys to the church, and the keys to our apartment building and our apartment. After telling me this, she promptly fainted. I managed to catch her and lay her down on the floor. I knelt beside her and said a fervent prayer for guidance, protection, and peace. I felt alone. Sister Monteiro came to about twenty seconds after my prayer ended. We went upstairs [to our neighbors' apartment] and began to deal with the situation.

"We used our neighbors' phone to call President's house and ask him to speak with the secretaries and have them cancel Sister Monteiro's mission credit card. President told us to call her home in Rio de Janeiro and cancel her personal card, which we did. Our neighbors were shocked to hear that we'd been robbed just then, because the husband said that he'd just gotten home—that he probably had arrived one minute earlier than we did. Also, there were about five police cars dealing with a traffic incident just around the corner from where we'd been robbed.

"We went back to our apartment and tried to get settled. We were worried because the robber had our keys, with the apartment number clearly marked. We were very unsettled and shaken. We deadbolted our bedroom door. To settle us a little more, we read [from] the Book of Mormon, and then prayed as usual. I asked Sister Monteiro if she had faith that the bag could be returned, and she said yes. I felt that I did too, so we prayed accordingly. I thought I would have trouble sleeping, but I didn't. I woke up a couple of times, and a part of me felt like panicking, but immediately a strong, sweet peace would fill me. I seemed to feel a heavenly presence in one corner of our room, and I felt very secure, and would fall back asleep quickly.

"When morning came, I felt sure we would find the bag just outside our apartment or on our street, but we found nothing. We went to Brasília, where I caught my bus for Cáceres. When I started working in Cáceres, I was jumpy. After dark, I couldn't concentrate very well because I was scared by every shadow. And in evaluating my deepest feelings, I realized that I was a little irritated with God and wondering why He allowed the robbery. He had warned me about it, and Sister Monteiro reported later that she, too, had felt that we would be robbed. Our neighbor had been there almost at the same time, and a whole crew of policemen had been less than 200 feet from the scene. It wouldn't have been that hard for Heavenly Father to prevent it . . . barely anything would have had to occur differently. I knew, from a sacred experience weeks earlier, that He really does exist and that He has all power and knowledge. What's more is that I had a powerful testimony of the protection of angels, as I had felt and witnessed it prior to this in my mission. So why had He let it happen? Was I unworthy of it? I knew that this question was undermining my faith and affecting my work, and I decided to resolve it.

"I knelt down to pray and explain my doubts and feelings. As I poured out my heart and tried to understand, my mind was opened. It wasn't my eyes that saw it, but the picture was very clear in my mind. I seemed to be standing on the other side of the street from our Taguatinga apartment watching the robbery. I saw Sister Monteiro struggling with the robber. About the time she let her bag go, I could see a shield of light, a protection, between us and the robber. I watched him and his companion run down the street, and that was the end of it. With this short scene came an outpouring of understanding to my mind and heart. I understood clearly, even more clearly than I saw, that we were protected. I understood the many ways we were protected: the robber didn't come into the apartment; he didn't take my bag (which allowed me to leave money with Sister Monteiro to cover her losses; had my bag been lost, we wouldn't have had that advantage); he didn't grab me, which would have probably been dangerous due to my assertive nature. I understood that He had warned us earlier for a number of reasons. We learned a little more about the voice of the Spirit. I also knew, because of the warning, that God knew it was coming and was in control the whole time. I don't know how to describe how clearly and quickly I understood Heavenly Father's love and protection. This was a powerful testimony of the living reality of a personal, loving, all-powerful God.

"This experience would be priceless if it ended there, but there are a few more details worth adding. I learned that Sister Monteiro's bag was found and returned the next day with everything in it except the camera. What a miracle, especially in Taguatinga! And Sister Monteiro later wrote to tell me another part of the story. Her older sister, who lives in Rio de Janeiro and pretty much raised Sister Monteiro, had been getting her family ready for bed on the evening of the robbery when she suddenly felt a very strong impression that she needed to pray for her sister. So she got down on her knees and prayed for her sister's safety and well-being. As she was getting up from her prayer, the phone rang. It was us, calling to cancel the stolen credit card of Sister Monteiro. Divine protection? There's no question. Oh, how great the goodness of our God!"

So what can we gather from these experiences? I recorded twenty-nine such occurrences of divine protection from the missionaries before I stopped chronicling them, but I have recited only a handful of examples here. Reviewing them side by side has helped me to come to some conclusions.

First, God and His emissaries have the power to provide whatever level of protection is needed, and can provide it quickly! They must be keenly aware of our circumstances—enough to come to our aid with split-second timing, in certain situations.

Second, God loves us, and He is kind. We may not always understand how certain circumstances can possibly be construed as kind; accidents sometimes do happen and God allows all mankind their agency. If accidents or man's agency place us in harm's way, and there is no divine intervention to prevent it, He will make it up to us and our loved ones, either in time or in eternity. His focus is not this life alone, but our eternal well-being. As the late Elder Joseph P. Wirthlin stated, "The Lord compensates the faithful for every loss. That which is taken away from those who love the Lord will be added unto them in His own way. While it may not come at the time we desire, the faithful will know that every tear today will eventually be returned a hundredfold with tears of rejoicing and gratitude."[6] Of this we can be sure.

I close with an experience of two missionaries who had an unexpected encounter with a night watchman. When they related it to me, it became personal.

Night Watchman

My wife and I returned from a trip to the city of Unaí in the state of Minas Gerais, where we had just recently established their first branch of the Church. Shortly after our arrival home on a warm, tropical Sunday evening, our two assistants came by to see us, and they were both clearly excited about something.

They related to us an experience they had at our home on the previous night. They had been working in the area and had dropped by at the end of the day to see whether we had already returned from Unaí. When they rang our doorbell, no one answered. The road was completely empty, which was normal at that hour in our community. What happened next was completely unexpected.

The elders explained how their attention was drawn to a man walking in their direction. At thirty meters away, his face was still unclear, but as he approached, the elders noticed his strange clothing—an open, heavy dark overcoat and a matching fedora hat that cast a shadow over his face as he passed below the glare of a streetlight. Elder Freire, a Brazilian, remarked that he had never seen that type of clothing on anyone in Brazil in his life—"only at the movies."

The man swayed slightly from side to side as he strolled toward the elders. "He did not seem to be walking like a human being," said Elder Freire. "He seemed to be almost floating." He moved down the street, specter-like, toward

6 Joseph P. Wirthlin "Come What May, and Love It," *Ensign*, Nov. 2008.

these two frightened missionaries. "That is not a man," Elder Freire told his companion.

As he drew nearer, the elders could make out his face with a soft, light glow to it. The hair that wasn't covered by the hat was dark brown. The man was nearly six feet tall, in his early thirties, and striking in his appearance. He never looked directly at the elders. They described the conversation that followed:

"Good evening. What are you looking for?" the man inquired in a friendly tone. He spoke in a very formal, archaic Portuguese found in the scriptures, with an accent characteristic of Rio Grande do Sul, the southernmost state of Brazil.

"We are looking for our president. Do you know him?" asked Elder Rampton.

"Yes, I do," he replied with a raised eyebrow and hint of a smile. "But he is not here. You can see that his automobile is not here." And with that, he continued walking toward a long sidewalk corridor near the mission home.

Elder Freire and his companion turned to each other and asked if the other felt something strange. "Each of us had felt a warmth of spirit as the man spoke with us, almost a loving feeling." Then they looked quickly to see where the man was going, but he was already gone—less than ten seconds from the time of his conversation with the elders.

After listening to the elders' account of what happened that night, I was still puzzled. "How could he have vanished?" I asked. The sidewalk corridor next to our house seemed too long for someone to walk in the time frame that the missionaries had described. Together with the elders, my wife and I retraced the man's steps along that corridor. It took us thirty-three seconds to get to the end of it, walking briskly, at which point the man could have turned and disappeared from sight. But the person they saw had less than ten seconds to do so before he disappeared. There was no place else where he could have gone. Moreover, I told the missionaries that I knew of no such man. Because we lived in a cloistered neighborhood, with tall, imposing, protective walls and high security gates, we had seen our neighbors only when they drove in and out of their automatic gates, and certainly none of them knew us.

I didn't know exactly how to interpret this, but knew that each night in our evening prayers we did ask God to "watch over our home" and undoubtedly, if the individual the missionaries met that night was sent to watch over our home, he would have known that the assistants posed no danger. His interaction with the missionaries would have been a gesture simply to let us know that our prayers were being attended. This was a significant comfort in our neighborhood, where houses on both sides of ours had been robbed recently. Our house, even without a watchdog, had been safe.

I thanked them for sharing their accounts and they left me to contemplate the experience. I walked slowly back into the house in deep thought. There were a number of strange details to consider. I recalled that prior to our departure for the mission, I had asked for a priesthood blessing from my uncle, who was serving as a patriarch in Akron, Ohio. One of the promises in that blessing was that my deceased father would be given permission to check up on our mission from time to time and help in the work. Remembering the blessing made me wonder whether the individual who spoke with Elder Freire and Elder Rampton was my father.

I returned to my mission home office and began thumbing through the few family photos that I had brought with me. I had one photo of my father in his mid-fifties, and four of him when he was thirty years old, taken when he accompanied Elder Ezra Taft Benson on a welfare mission shortly after World War II. As I viewed them, I noticed for the first time that in all four photos, my father was wearing a heavy dark overcoat and a matching fedora hat. In each photo he appeared to be smiling directly at me. My father was five feet, ten and a half inches in height. A "warm chill" (if there is such a sensation) ran up my spine as I pondered the divine signature.

The photo above shows my father (center, rear) surrounded by the five junior apostles who accompanied him to the airport as he and Elder Benson departed for their humanitarian mission to war-torn Europe in January 1946. From left to right, Elder Matthew Cowley, Elder Spencer W. Kimball, Elder Harold B. Lee, Frederick W. Babbel, Elder Ezra Taft Benson, and Elder Mark E. Petersen.

About a year later and after our missions had concluded, Elder Rampton pulled me aside and spoke with me privately. He said that he had been thinking about that nighttime visitor. "Was your father an outgoing man?" he asked.

"Yes, he was very outgoing," I said. "In fact, he would frequently start up conversations with strangers in elevators . . . even in New York City! Why do you ask?"

Elder Rampton continued, "I believe the [outgoing] man that we saw that night was your father. I think that I know why your father spoke to us in Portuguese. My companion did not speak a word of English, but I was able to converse in either language, so this man spoke in a way that we both could understand." I hadn't said anything about my father in connection with the night watchman incident to the elders, and was pleasantly surprised that his conclusion aligned with mine.

Chapter 5

BLESSINGS, ORDINANCES, AND PRIESTHOOD

> *Therefore, in the ordinances thereof, the power of godliness is manifest.*
>
> D&C 84:20

Missionaries are relatively new to administering the ordinances of the priesthood, and because of this, they sometimes focus on the formalities of the ordinances. I understand this tendency, and I know I did the same as a new elder. I've noticed, though, that when we focus on the formalities, it's easier to miss the divine power that undergirds and accompanies the rituals.

Some of the missionaries recorded times when they were able to look beyond the formalities, drawing back the curtain and witnessing the true heavenly nature of the ordinances. These experiences strengthened their testimonies of the efficacy and divinity of the ordinances.

Over the course of a very short time, I collected twenty-one reports that revealed how some missionaries had been permitted to see or feel the holy sanction given to such ordinances. I share six of them here, in the hope that they will help give us a glimpse of the sacred power behind these functions.

Confirmation Ordinance

Elder Nunes wrote me from Formosa of an experience he had while confirming Dona Juracy (pseudonym), a member of the Church. Dona Juracy was a woman in her early sixties who had to overcome heavy smoking and deep resentment in preparation for her baptism. My translation of a portion of his letter follows.

"I was given the privilege of performing this ordinance, and I knew that it was a very sacred moment for her. Because of this I was tempted to begin thinking of and storing up in my mind some words that I should pronounce during the [confirmation] blessing. But I had the clear feeling that I should not do this, but should instead pray in my mind for spiritual guidance and inspiration in what I should say. Indeed, that is what I did, saying a number of silent prayers before performing the ordinance.

"When I placed my hands upon her head, I felt a calmness and tranquility and knew that I could put my confidence in the Lord. I don't remember the majority of things that I spoke in the blessing, but I was left with no doubts that what I said was what the Lord wanted me to say, and that I made promises and blessed her in the way the Lord wanted me to do. The Spirit was so strong!

"When we removed our hands from the head of Dona Juracy, she had tears running down her cheeks and cried for a long time. At the end of Sacrament Meeting she told me that she felt something unlike anything she had ever felt before. During the ordinance, her life passed before her mind like a movie, and she felt clearly at that moment that everything amiss was forgotten, and that a completely new life had begun. It was then that I gained a real and profound understanding of how a person, even though older, could truly be born again."

He continued, "Dona Juracy understood that she would not necessarily receive a manifestation of the presence of the Holy Ghost at her confirmation, but said, 'I know that I did receive the Holy Ghost today!' I also know! The Spirit was so strong during and after the confirmation that I also was unable to withhold my tears.

"I have already confirmed several people in the past, some of whom had a manifestation of the Spirit, but never before have I witnessed the power of the Holy Ghost acting so strongly and deeply as in the case of this humble woman.

He added, "I felt so happy with all of this that I just wanted to share this joy with you, President, who were the main instrument in the hands of the Lord."

Elder Nunes's selfless comment at the end of his letter claiming that I was somehow instrumental in Dona Juracy's baptism was based on my contribution of some gospel reading material to her. I gave a copy of the "Dissolving Resentments" essay[7] to Dona Juracy to prepare her for baptism. That chapter had a miraculous effect upon her, and she underwent a complete repentance process prior to her baptism.

7 This is a chapter in *To Him That Believeth*, by Frederick W. Babbel (Bookcraft, 1980). This volume was republished by Cedar Fort, Inc., in 1997.

More than anything, I appreciated Elder Nunes's inspiration that he should not plan the words of the confirmation blessing ahead of time, but rather seek through earnest prayer to be able to say the words that the Lord would have him say in the ordinance. This trust in the Holy Ghost helped both Elder Nunes and Dona Juracy to feel the strong presence of the Lord's Spirit during the confirmation. Elder Nunes undertook a preparation that led to this turning point for Dona Juracy. I doubt that the experience would have been as powerful if Dona Juracy had not also prepared by dissolving the deep resentments she had long been harboring.

Baptismal Power

Sister Monteiro was a missionary from Rio de Janeiro who studied Greek and other ancient languages in college prior to her mission. She was able to witness the power of the baptismal ordinance, and she later wrote me a letter about it:

"It began as a normal baptism, with the small children causing a commotion, as always. A very special moment occurred when Elder Snell entered into the waters to baptize Wesley. I saw him enveloped in a column of light, with a whiteness that is indescribable. He looked like an angel of the Lord. At that moment I felt the power of God in that ordinance; I had never seen anything like it before. I instantly felt the Spirit confirming that baptism is the gate that opens into the Celestial Kingdom. I knew about this, perhaps more as something obvious, but never in this manner. I felt as if my heart were catching on fire. I could not contain the joy that I felt, nor control the tears. Really, I felt that this ordinance was true."

House Dedication

We encouraged missionaries and members to dedicate their places of abode. Our hope was that the dedications would buttress the members and missionaries against the power of the adversary and allow them to feel the Lord's presence more in their homes. The following account from Elder Araújo and Elder Parronchi is a sample of what resulted.

"President, it is marvelous to feel the Spirit guiding and helping us at all times. I am grateful to be able to serve a mission.

"This week we had the opportunity to see that we are engaged in a true work. We were at the home of inactive members. We had gone there to dedicate their home.

"When we arrived there that night, we looked into the rooms and saw that they were very dark. After offering the dedicatory prayer, the Spirit was present and very strong, and when we looked at the rooms, we both saw that they were very bright and filled with light. Truly, the Spirit was purifying that house!

"It was very gratifying to witness this, and this is yet another reason that I love this work and this mission."

A Comfort Blessing

Elder Lavelli included the following paragraph in one of his weekly letters to me.

"A recent convert [Maurício] asked for a blessing of comfort and then, before doing it, I offered a prayer in my mind asking that the Spirit speak through me so that the Lord could use me as an instrument in His hands. Then, when I placed my hands upon Maurício's head and began to state the authority, I had the complete certainty that I was led by the Spirit because I don't remember the words I spoke. All I know is that I became tired to the point of having to breathe deeply to recuperate. I have never had something like this so strong before, and I know with all of the understanding that has been given to me that the power of the priesthood is sacred and if we call upon the help of the Holy Ghost, the Lord will send Him and He will speak through us at all times."

The subject of healings is dealt with in depth later on in this book, particularly in the chapter about the Faith Conference. But two instances of health blessings have been included here because these particular accounts focus on the *experience* of the blessing more than anything else. They show that giving a priesthood blessing can lead to an unimaginably glorious experience for the priesthood bearer. Truly, the priesthood can unlock amazing things.

Blessing an Investigator

Elder Tolentino was fairly new on his mission. He and his companion felt inspired to track down referrals, and while they were out, a woman invited them into her home. She wanted the elders to meet her husband, who was bedridden because of a lung disease. They followed her to the room, where they saw her husband breathing with the help of an oxygen mask.

"She began to weep a lot to see her husband in such a state," Elder Tolentino wrote, "and after we read a Biblical passage from James 5:14–15, we pronounced a blessing of health upon her husband.

"As the blessing was being administered, I felt a strong desire that the man be cured. I wanted to take his place to suffer what he was suffering. At that moment, I felt a very strong warmth in my heart, [and] as if a third set of hands were upon ours. I felt the Lord blessing that man. The impression that I had was so touching that it appeared that my feet were not even touching the ground.

"At the conclusion of the blessing, I was unable to withhold my tears. My sobbing broke the silence. The woman of the house was emotional and asked that we return on another occasion to her home. I know that I was an instrument in the hands of the Lord to bless the life of that man at that moment. My testimony about the priesthood was reinforced and renewed. Oh, how I am grateful to Heavenly Father to be a bearer of this precious gift!"

Vision during a Blessing

(In the case of this final story, the names have been changed to respect the privacy of those who had the experience.)

Migraine headaches plagued Elder Taylor during his mission. They typically would last for several hours or even days, and sometimes they debilitated him to the point that he could not work. The following account comes from his missionary companion, Elder Barbosa, who was full of faith. The blessing given demonstrates that sometimes, when the Spirit inspires the blessing, unexpected things can happen.

"On Preparation Day, Elder Taylor began to have a very strong migraine headache. He was in very bad condition, and had already taken medicine but the pain was increasing. He then came to me and said, 'Elder Barbosa, place your hands on my head and give me a blessing and cure me.'

"I could sense the great faith that he had, so I attended to his request. In that blessing I had a vision of the premortal existence, where we were together and I was given a certainty that our companionship had been foreordained. The Spirit was very strong and the two of us wept. I was able to rebuke the pain, and he was immediately cured. What a great testimony of the power, the work, and the love of our Father in Heaven."

I noted two things about this blessing. First, Elder Taylor demonstrated faith by not just asking for a blessing, but by asking to be cured. Certainly his faith was such that if given a blessing to be cured, he would be cured, and he was—immediately! Second, I was touched that in the vision of the premortal existence, the elder giving the blessing saw that he was meant to serve with his companion. This was not the only case of missionaries telling me that they knew their companionship was foreordained, but in this case, the knowledge was accompanied by a vision. Elder Barbosa saw many other things during that vision of a most sacred nature.

It showed me once again that these ordinances are not of this earth and that the priesthood is nothing short of the power to act in the Lord's name. I was grateful these missionaries were able to see that too.

Chapter 6

OBEDIENCE: TO WHAT? TO WHOM?

> *Then Peter and the other apostles answered and said, We ought to obey God rather than men.*
>
> Acts 5:29

The first few chapters in this book show missionaries learning to rely on the Lord in many ways: to gain a testimony, to communicate, to avoid danger, and to respect the sacred nature of ordinances. These are important matters to all of the Lord's servants, but especially to new ones. Once missionaries settle in, though, they still need the Lord's help. The work of finding people to teach and knowing what to say—topics that are covered in the next few chapters—is much more successful when a missionary is obedient to the promptings of the Holy Ghost. Obedience to the Lord and His counsel can require courage.

The Spirit of Contention

Some missionaries learn about obedience the hard way. I placed two elders (who will remain unnamed) together in a companionship after they had driven the rest of their companions crazy by constantly quarreling with them. Although they were both wonderful and valiant men, they didn't adapt well to working in companionships. I had the faint hope that these two missionaries would recognize their own harmful behavior when they saw it in each other and make amends, but in the more likely case that this didn't happen, at least I would be containing the fallout to a single companionship.

It didn't take long for the elders to report to me that things weren't working out between them. Matters came to a head one evening when they called and told me that their situation had reached the breaking point. I counseled them that the spirit of contention was incompatible with having the Holy Spirit (3 Ne. 11:29) and that "if ye receive not the Spirit, ye shall not teach" (D&C 42:14). This was not just a suggestion, I told them, because they could actually do harm if they continued to represent the Lord while harboring such ill feelings toward each other. I instructed them to forgo any proselytizing or member visits until they could get along. They were to stay in their apartment and fill their time with personal study and prayer or with activities that did not necessarily require the Spirit, like cleaning.

Sure enough, the next morning the two elders ignored my advice and went out to proselytize. When they returned home for lunch, their apartment had been ransacked. About half of their belongings were gone, including their cameras, their money, and some clothing. They called me (collect) to ask what they should do.

"How could this have happened?" I asked. "I told you to stay home." They explained to me that they simply could not justify remaining in their apartment when there was missionary work to be done. I applauded the sentiment, but still felt that they needed to iron out their companionship problems first. Once again, I counseled them to stay at home until they could work together in harmony.

The elders continued to bicker with each other, yet they decided to go back on the road for missionary work that afternoon. When they returned to their apartment that night, they were shocked. It had been ransacked again! This time *everything* was gone. They called me that night (again, collect) to explain. Their furniture and bedding were gone. Even their underwear and scriptures had been stolen. Their apartment was completely empty!

It was hard for me to believe that they had so readily ignored counsel, even after the first break-in. I made provision for them to get some supplies the next day, but they had to sleep on the floor that night.

This story exemplifies how important it is for missionaries to carefully consider the counsel of their leaders, which will most probably result in compliance. The next example is one in which the missionaries also sought my advice, but upon prayerful reflection, decided to go another direction, to their ultimate blessing. The principle I've learned after reflecting on these two stories is that the Lord is the one who has called these missionaries to serve, not their stake president, bishop, or mission president, and their first allegiance must be to the Lord if a conflict in counsel arises.

Lack of Vision?

Elder Reid was a powerful and reflective missionary. He was one who always sought to do his best and to live in such a way that he could enjoy the companionship of the Holy Spirit, which would help direct him in the work and also impress upon his investigators the truthfulness of the gospel message. He was one of those missionaries who exemplified what was said of Moroni: "[I]f all men had been, and were, and ever would be, like unto Moroni, behold, the very powers of hell would have been shaken forever; yea, the devil would never have power over the hearts of the children of men" (Alma 48:17). He was serving in the Federal District when he developed a severe problem. The following is taken verbatim from a journal entry that his companion, Elder Rampton, wrote and shared with me:

"Last week, Elder Reid had developed a corneal ulcer in his right eye. We had to leave the mission conference early on the 24th. By that day, he'd been in pain for almost a week (red swelling, throbbing eye). We left conference and as we got back to Sobradinho, I decided he needed to go to the hospital. (Before leaving conference I'd given him a blessing that he would be healed, and thus know the power of the Priesthood, amongst other counsel and blessings.) Well, I called Paulo, one of the brethren of the local congregation who worked in the emergency room. He was awaiting our arrival and got us in the front of the line. In a room completely full of waiting patients, we waited only five minutes. However, the doctor was unable to do much, saying that we needed a specialist, the nearest one being back in Brasília. The doctor was unable to do anything to soothe Elder Reid's pain, as any pain-killing drops would mask the ophthalmologist's diagnosis. This then left us debating what to do.

"We had no car to get us to Brasília [about 15 miles distant], and no members were available. Brother Paulo said he could set us up with an ambulance, but there were only two on call, so it was risky to leave only one ambulance at the hospital's disposal in case of emergency. Needless to say, Elder Reid was in no condition to take a bus.

"I called President Babbel to seek his advice. He said we ought not go to the hospital in Brasília because it would be full of drunkards on that Brazilian holiday and no specialist would attend us. He said, 'Take him home, have him close his eye and get some rest.'

"Well, I related the advice to Elder Reid, who agreed. However, Brother Paulo wouldn't have it. He double checked, and found out that there were now three available ambulances. He insisted that we take one to Brasília. I said, 'Elder Reid, it's your health, you make the call.' He was slightly indecisive, but we coaxed each other into the old ambulance, accompanied by Brother Paulo. On the way to the hospital my phone rang. The caller I.D. showed 'President Babbel.' Before answering, I said, 'Elder Reid, it's for you!'

"Well, Elder Reid answered and explained that we had decided to go against the President's advice, and were already on the way to Brasília. I'm not sure how President reacted. We got to the hospital, and with the aid of Brother Paulo, we were quickly attended to without any complications. (If we had gone to the normal private hospital with which the mission has a contract, we would have been up to our ears in paperwork, phone calls, faxes, etc. before being attended.) The woman ophthalmologist started off by giving Elder Reid some miracle eye drop. After the exam, he was diagnosed with a corneal ulcer [i.e., bacteria eating a hole into his eye, caused by infection from him leaving his contact lenses in too long and overnight]. There was only a razor thin tissue remaining to protect his inner eye. Had he waited one more day, she said, the bacteria would have completely eaten a hole in his eye and penetrated the cornea. He was prescribed eye drops to use every hour on the hour.[8]

"By the next day, President set up a consultation with a member of the Church who was a well-known ophthalmologist, Air Force Capitão Geraldo. He gave Elder Reid the same diagnosis, only worse! He prescribed the same eye drops and said that he should stay away from all light. The president put him up in the mission home, where he had a room to himself, in complete darkness.

"After a couple of days of listening to talks on CDs, Elder Reid's hunger for literature overcame him. He read for a while on the subject of faith. He said at that point his eye was still swollen, red and throbbing. He went to put more eye drops in. As he went into the bathroom to use the sink, he recalled certain words pronounced to him in the blessing that I [Elder Rampton] had given him. The Lord had counseled him to wash his eye out. (Elder Reid knows the counsel better than I, as I remember little to none of the words I pronounced during the blessing.)

"Well, Elder Reid was conflicted, as both doctors told him not to wash his eye out with water. He pondered over the sink, in front of the mirror for a minute, put the fear behind him, and washed out the eye with water. As soon as he did, he looked in the mirror and saw the redness dissipating. From that moment on, his eye began to heal quickly.

"After we checked back with Capitão Geraldo, we realized what a miracle it was. In less than a week (Thursday to Wednesday), Elder Reid had a miraculous 95% recovery, the normal recovery time being a period of 20–40 days, with a 20-day minimum. This faithful doctor, also a firm member, assured us that the

8 I have since learned that a corneal ulcer is a medical emergency which requires immediate medical attention and frequent topical antibiotics to prevent the ulcer from perforating through the cornea. A perforated corneal ulcer is a medical disaster which can severely damage the eye and even cause blindness very rapidly.

Lord had His hand in this recovery and must have something special in store for Elder Reid. The doctor said that with such little time left on Elder Reid's mission, he was ready to send him home had he not recovered so quickly."

Obviously, my advice wasn't very good on this occasion, but I can take some satisfaction in what I taught all of my missionaries at the outset of their missions. I taught them that I, as their president, would give them my best efforts to provide wise counsel, yet despite my best efforts, I would undoubtedly make mistakes. If they felt sure through the Spirit that my counsel was in error, then the Spirit should always take precedence. Had I not taught that principle, Elder Reid would have been less likely to make the decision to rush to the hospital that night, in variance with my recommendations. I never criticized any missionary for following the Spirit in good faith.

I'm also impressed that Elder Reid recognized inspired counsel, which in this case came through the blessing that Elder Rampton pronounced. Because Elder Reid had the courage to follow this inspiration, he made a miraculous recovery.

I've learned that while faith and obedience are vital principles, they must be rooted in the correct source. It is not faith alone, but "faith in the Lord Jesus Christ" that saves, not obedience alone, but "obedience to God" that blesses us and others.

Chapter 7

UNCOMFORTABLE PROMPTINGS

A person may profit by noticing the first intimation of the spirit of revelation . . . those things that were presented unto your minds by the Spirit of God, will come to pass.

Joseph Smith, in *History of the Church*, 3:381

Obedience to God, of course, is not always easy. Sometimes it can be downright uncomfortable. I received many accounts from the missionaries about promptings that impelled them to do something awkward or counterintuitive, usually related to talking to a stranger about the gospel. The missionaries learned through trial and error how to identify inspiration and why it was important to quickly heed these promptings.

To "Bug" Her or Not to "Bug" Her

Sister Ward and her companion were buying food at a bakery when their nametags caught the attention of a female employee. The woman was curious about the sisters and the work they did, so Sister Ward explained their role. Immediately, the woman said she'd love for the missionaries to visit her at her house. She said she was searching for the word of God and was feeling very alone living far away from her family. She had moved to the area eight months before with her husband but was now separated from him.

Sister Ward wrote, "As I was talking with her I felt the Spirit so strongly! I really wanted to teach her at that very moment so she could have more happiness in her life and could find the light of Christ. I took down her address and left, then returned quickly to schedule a time with her. Our schedules didn't combine until almost a week later. I was sad because I wanted to teach her quickly. I wanted to move things around so we could teach her sooner. But we left.

"Later that day I kept feeling like we should invite her to Church the next day so we could start with her sooner, but we'd already returned there once and I didn't want to 'bug' her or something. Anyway, we did go to her house one day earlier than the scheduled visit to confirm that we would be there, but as we arrived there the owner of the house told us that she'd moved back home to Bahia two days earlier. When I heard this I was crushed and so ashamed that I didn't listen to the Spirit. I felt horrible. This was a really good lesson to me. When the Spirit is telling you something, don't wait; just do it. Even if you just have a thought about doing something, more than likely that's how the Spirit is talking to you."

This story illustrates a common human reaction to the direction of the Spirit. We often second-guess the impression and try to figure out how to brush it aside conveniently. In this case, the perfectly reasonable rationale not to invite the investigator to Church was that "we'd already returned there once and I didn't want to 'bug' her." Sometimes, perhaps more often than we think, the adversary may put such seemingly logical thoughts into our minds. But whether the thoughts come from us or from below, they do not outweigh the promptings of the Spirit.

The next account comes from Elder Anjos, who reacted quickly to a prompting. I no longer have a copy of his original letter, but his experience was so singular that I am including my wife's and my recollection of it, which he reviewed and approved.

Do Not Use This Question!?

Elder Anjos was contacting people on the street when he suddenly felt the desire to ask a certain man, about sixty years old, an unusual question: "Why do you think that the ordinance of baptism for the dead is not practiced among most of Christianity today?" Once the words left his mouth, the question surprised Elder Anjos himself. He had never opened a conversation like this before, and he wondered how such a question could possibly promote this stranger's interest in the gospel. Indeed, several months earlier at a zone conference, a visiting member of the Area Presidency had taught us that this was exactly the type of question that we should *avoid*, as it might foster more negative intrigue than positive. Still, Elder Anjos said that he felt the Spirit leading him to bring up the subject with this individual.

The man responded that he was Pastor Jairo of a local protestant church. He told Elder Anjos that he had long been searching for the true church of Jesus Christ, which he felt would surely have such an ordinance today, as it did in times past. Needless to say, Elder Anjos was even more startled at the man's response than he was at his initial question about vicarious ordinances. Pastor Jairo then invited him and his companion to his home to explain more about the Church.

On their first two visits to his home, Pastor Jairo's behavior was rude and contentious to the elders. They were surprised that on their third visit, he apologized to the missionaries, saying that he was testing them to see whether they were true representatives of Jesus Christ, for he felt that representatives of the true Church would not retaliate, but would be humble and longsuffering. Since the elders had passed his little test with flying colors, he promised to be more civil in the future and asked to receive the missionary lessons. The elders were quite relieved that the pastor's negative behavior was a test, and they were even more relieved to realize that they had passed the test.

Pastor Jairo and his family soon heard all of the messages from the missionaries. He and his family gained testimonies and were baptized. Pastor Jairo became a valiant, leading member of the local branch and was soon sustained as a counselor to the branch president. Within his community he became a powerful force for good as well as an outstanding missionary.

When I reflect on this incident, I can see that the Lord knows his children. He knows what they need to come closer to him, and in this case, Pastor Jairo needed to hear about vicarious ordinances for the dead. Elder Anjos acted on this prompting, trusting that the Spirit knew better than he how to reach this man. Had Elder Anjos resisted the inspiration, I doubt that Pastor Jairo would have ever felt inclined to listen to the young elders, much less invite them to his home.

Balk

A new missionary, Elder Neves, listened as Elder Anjos shared the story about Pastor Jairo at a zone conference. Elder Neves then stood up and told us about a prompting he had received while making a contact, only with a different ending to the story.

While waiting at a bus stop, Elder Neves felt directed to contact the woman who was also waiting there. He didn't feel prompted to make just an ordinary contact, however. The feeling came with specific instructions: he was to speak to her about the doctrine of the resurrection.

Elder Neves was taken aback by the idea—what kind of nutcase would make small talk with a stranger at a bus stop about resurrection? He decided to stay quiet and not risk embarrassment.

His senior companion, Elder Parronchi, began conversing with this same woman while waiting for the bus. She immediately responded by saying that she'd always had trouble understanding the doctrine of the resurrection, and she wondered whether Elder Parronchi could explain his understanding of the doctrine to her.

After speaking of this experience at our zone conference, Elder Neves later lamented the missed opportunity in a letter. "I could hear the voice of the Spirit; however, I did not discern it to be so but thought that it was merely something coming from my own head. Afterward, the Lord showed me that it really was His voice that had spoken to me in my mind." Had he followed the initial promptings of the Spirit, this woman would have received a witness at the outset that the elders were indeed representatives of Jesus Christ, because they would have approached her with the very thing that had troubled her over the years. Elder Neves went on to say, "I need to learn to discern better." He resolved not to ignore such promptings in the future.

Most missionaries learn with difficulty how to discern the whisperings of the Spirit from the thoughts that originate within the person's own mind. It is a struggle, but a vital one.

Not all promptings lead to proselyting ends. The Spirit inspired the missionaries to do good in many ways, some of which led to saving ordinances, like baptism, and others that didn't. I observed that the Lord's vision of the good that missionaries could do was often broader than my own. The next two stories come from missionaries who felt they had to warn somebody about something. The first of these experiences was recorded in a letter by Sister Almeida, who was walking along a road with her two companions when a stranger caught her attention.

Whisperings for an Alcoholic

"As we passed [the stranger], I felt a strong spiritual prompting that I should talk to the man and tell him not to go drinking. I thought the impression was so strange that it could be offensive, and must not be of God. I supposed that the thought had originated in my own mind, although it seemed rather strange for me to concoct. As we passed by him, the thought came again, but stronger. I again began to doubt the wisdom of telling a man not to drink while contacting him when he was unknown to us and was not drinking. So we continued on our way. Moments later the thought came to me again, but more urgently. 'Tell the man that you are God's messengers, and that if he goes drinking, he will die.' I felt that the thought, albeit uncomfortable, must be of God, for I would never have thought of doing such a thing.

Sister Almeida continued, "I informed my companions [she was in a threesome at the time] that I felt a prompting that we should turn around and contact that man who had passed us earlier. They didn't argue, so we went in search of him. He had already walked some distance and was walking with another man. The three of us ran back to speak with him. I introduced us to him, and told him that I wasn't sure why I should say it, but that he should not go drinking or he would die. The feeling was so strong that it appeared as if it were not I who was speaking. He looked very surprised (as did his friend), and confessed that he had just been discharged from the hospital and was headed to the bar to go drinking with his friend.[9] He asked us if we were messengers from God. He left his friend and began to walk back with us in the direction where we had been headed earlier. I was concerned whether he would hear and obey the words that the Lord had prompted me to tell him. He asked us a number of questions about our faith and decided not to go drinking on that occasion. I don't know what happened to him afterward, for I was transferred shortly thereafter.

"It showed to me how God is anxious to use us as His messengers to His other children, and that He is caring for all. As uncomfortable as it was for me to make a contact by delivering such an abrupt warning, I am glad that I had the courage to follow the Spirit and give him that vital message."

Vision after a Street Contact

"I had a peculiar experience with following the Spirit near the end of my mission," wrote a missionary of ours after he had returned home. "Early one afternoon, as I was walking past the Ministries Esplanade situated in front of the Senate and Congress buildings in Brasília, I encountered a young couple among about a dozen people standing at a bus stop. The young man was around nineteen and his girlfriend perhaps seventeen. They were waiting for a bus. The girl was dressed somewhat immodestly and was being flirtatious with the young man. As I passed by, the Spirit whispered to me to return and speak to the couple. I turned my companion around and we introduced ourselves. As we began to converse, The Spirit whispered for us to teach them about the Word

9 A medical doctor later reviewed this account and offered the following insight: "There is a very large list of medications often given in the hospital that do not mix well with alcohol. Any anesthetic (for instance, if the person had an outpatient procedure been done that day) should be followed by the instructions not to drink alcohol for 24 hours because of the potential deleterious effect of the combination. The same is true of most narcotics given in the hospital for pain, and any anti-anxiety medications. There is a list of many medications that can be harmful if ingested along with alcohol or other substances. If one starts mixing chemicals that shouldn't be mixed, it can result in death. My assumption is that the Lord knew whatever had happened at the hospital could be lethal in combination with a binge drink of alcohol and wanted to extend this person's life."

of Wisdom. I felt it was somewhat awkward to begin a contact in that manner, but I followed 'orders' in the best way I could. I followed another prompting to invite them to live the Word of Wisdom, and the girl said that she would, while the young man nodded his assent.

"Then, after a short pause, the Spirit washed over me in an urgent manner and impelled me to explain to them the Law of Chastity and tell them they must not break this important law. I was rather startled about this whole episode because that is not the usual way a missionary conducts a first contact! Nonetheless, the impression was sufficiently strong that I did not hesitate, so after identifying ourselves as messengers of Jesus Christ, I explained to them the Law of Chastity and told them that they must not break the Law of Chastity, as well as the Word of Wisdom. The girl agreed, but the young man was noncommittal. I received an impression through the Spirit that they were on their way to a house or apartment of a friend.

"The girl and her boyfriend were both rather taken aback, yet the girl stood and announced proudly that in spite of being seventeen years old, she had maintained her virginity. Brazil is a wonderful country with even more marvelous people, but in my observation, one characteristic inherent to their culture is a trend among the youth to break the Law of Chastity at an early age. That she was so old and still living this law was surprising. Her boyfriend was rather defensive about the affront, but gave a half-hearted commitment at the end. Among the 9–12 people at the bus stop, it is likely that several of them were listening to the conversation. The Spirit was abnormally strong during that conversation, and I was sure that the couple had felt it, particularly the girl. Her eyes were transfixed upon us as the messages were delivered.

"I congratulated them, and then bid them farewell. Later that evening, roughly three hours after the conversation, as I was walking back to our apartment, I had a vision quickly pop into my mind of the young couple, faces both turned down toward the ground in sadness and shame, having just broken the Law. I remember vividly the pained expression on the girl's face, being horror-struck emotionally just as she had broken the Law. It was extremely disconcerting and depressing for me to see those images, as she had committed to live the Law only hours earlier, and we had tried with such zeal to encourage them to do so. I felt badly that they had not abided by the counsel from the Lord that I was bidden to convey. I grieved for them both. However, after my immediate reaction of heartfelt sorrow, I felt peace come to my heart, and I knew that the Lord could teach her through the stark contrast of the feelings she had earlier that day with what she later felt. This thought comforted me and gave me hope for her in the future."

I was proud of the missionary in this example for his willingness to follow the Spirit, even if it meant breaking a few taboos in conversation. Given how sensitive he was toward the feelings of others and how non-confrontational he was by nature, I knew this was a real test for him. His account also showed me how God watches over all of His children and He wanted this particular couple to be warned before they sinned. Surely this warning will stay in the minds of the young couple and later inure to their benefit.

The examples about uncomfortable promptings remind me of cases in the scriptures. Certainly, Jonah, Lehi, Jeremiah, Isaiah, Alma, Paul, Samuel the Lamanite, and many others were at times uneasy with their assignments to cry repentance. They didn't always see fruit from their efforts because their listeners could choose to heed or ignore the call to repentance. Still, by God's standard, each messenger was successful when she or he faithfully delivered the intended message.

Besides helping others, promptings can help the missionary receiving them. The following story comes from Sister Inouye and Sister Monteiro, who were brilliant scholars prior to their missions, but also just about the shyest two missionaries I ever knew. I was amazed at the way the Spirit emboldened and transformed them in this experience, since these two sisters were the last people I would ever expect to try such a thing!

Singing in Assembly of God Church

"The other day Sister Inouye and I had a few moments of time available between an appointment and our scheduled tracting," wrote Sister Monteiro in a letter. "Sister Inouye was curious and had a desire to enter into a large Assembly of God chapel in our area that was nearby. We entered it and found it absolutely loaded with people. That day was a type of conference for pastors from various states across Brazil, and the program featured several special musical numbers, with the women chicly dressed in the kind of garb usually seen at weddings. We removed our nametags to avoid any repercussions from our attendance.

"I said to my companion, 'Let's go up in front and sing for them.' My companion got very nervous and scared and did not want to do that. Then a question came to my heart: 'Who are you? Are you ashamed of Christ?' I knew at that moment that we should put our nametags back on. The pastor giving the sermon then asked if there were people visiting from other churches.

"I introduced us to the congregation, and we stood up and stated that we were missionaries from The Church of Jesus Christ of Latter-day Saints. There was no retaliation. I then said to my companion, 'Let's sing for them, Sister. I would like these people to all have the opportunity to feel the Spirit!' I then went to the front near the pulpit, and asked permission for us to sing to them. The woman near the pulpit said to us, 'Ah, the pastor would have to authorize it and we already have a program to follow.' But then, out of the blue, they announced that we would sing for them.

"We sang the hymn 'Nearer My God to Thee.' I don't sing with a pretty voice, but I asked the Lord to help me have a beautiful voice only at that moment. I was nervous and shaking. We sang into the microphone and knew that our music would probably be heard from blocks away, because it is always possible to hear the electronically amplified preaching and music in this church from a great distance away. It was one of the most beautiful hymns I have ever heard. I announced in the microphone who we were. At that moment, the Spirit was there and came upon us. I looked about us and we were encircled with light. The congregation could really feel the Holy Ghost for several minutes. It was an incredible experience. I am so grateful to be a representative of Jesus Christ."

The following story happened repeatedly, in various degrees and situations, to many of the missionaries. I take this particular account from a report of Elder Silva, who worked with Elder Homer.

Stopped in My Tracks

"My companion and I were on our way to an appointment. While we were walking there, we were conversing about the needs of our investigators. All at once, we saw a woman in the distance sitting on the sidewalk curb with her young son. I felt that she was crying, and that we should speak with her! But then I thought, well, if she is crying the last thing she would want is to be bothered by some rabid religious type of person, as we are perceived. As I let this thought guide me, the Spirit stopped my legs and I turned and began to walk in the direction of that woman . . .

"Upon reaching her we greeted her and introduced ourselves. She looked at us with her eyes full of tears, and trembling somewhat she asked us: 'Who are you?' We responded, 'We are messengers of Jesus Christ, and we feel that we should speak with you.' She responded, 'I am very sad and very confused. My husband abandoned me, and even the church that I attended looks upon me with apprehension and distrust. I just got finished praying to God that he would illuminate the path I should follow and show me a church. And He has responded to me by putting you two men of light in my path.' She said many other things and even bore her testimony after we taught her.

"This experience was a good one. She already knows that the Book of Mormon is true and will be attending our church next Sunday."

The final two accounts both involve buses, the main source of transportation for the missionaries. I learned that when a bus schedule seems to stand in the way of doing the Lord's errand, it's best to leave the schedule behind!

A Bus to the Rescue

I heard the following story from the elders themselves after they returned to Brasília, and Elder Crossen later confirmed all the details for me before I recorded them in writing.

At the conclusion of a zone conference in the state of Tocantins, Elders Crossen and Cardoso, who were serving as my assistants at that time, took the local bus over to the regional bus station to catch their long bus ride back to Brasília. They had in their pockets their previously purchased bus tickets for a sixteen-hour trip to Brasília that was scheduled to leave Palmas at six o'clock in the evening.

As they approached within two blocks of the bus station, Elder Crossen felt impressed to get off the local bus and visit Sister Marli, who was popularly regarded as the "mission mother" in that area. He told Elder Cardoso that they should get off the bus and visit her, but Elder Cardoso thought the idea was a little crazy. It was turning six o'clock at that very moment, and they were likely to miss their bus connection to Brasília if they visited the woman.

Nonetheless, Elder Crossen stood by the prompting, which he felt was divine. He insisted that they both exit the local bus at that time and walk over to Sister Marli's house. Elder Cardoso consented, so they pulled the bus cord and the driver stopped near Marli's house.

The elders paid her a brief visit. Sister Marli was too ill to get out of bed, so they spoke with her at her bedside. They learned that she was suffering from dengue fever, a tropical mosquito-borne disease that debilitates its victims, oftentimes killing them if left untreated. She told the elders that the local members had not visited her at all during the course of her illness, which had left her feeling depressed. The elders' visit lifted her spirits and gave her courage to continue with the lengthy recovery process.

After the elders left Marli's home, they ran to the regional bus station, heavy backpacks in tow. Elder Crossen was sure that the bus would still be there waiting, even though the departure time had already passed. But once they drew close to the regional bus station, they saw the six o'clock bus pulling away and entering the highway. They had no way of catching up or signaling for the bus to stop.

Elder Crossen did not understand why the bus had left. After all, he and Elder Cardoso had been on the Lord's errand. Surely, he thought, the Lord would reward them with a way to catch the bus back to mission headquarters!

He asked the station agent at the ticket office whether there was any other bus going that day to Brasília. The agent looked at the schedule and said that there was one other bus scheduled to leave for Brasília hours earlier, but that it had been delayed in arriving from Belém (over one thousand miles away) and would arrive in Palmas within twenty minutes. He said that they could even use their same pre-purchased tickets, although this second bus would take a much faster route to Brasília and arrive there by six o'clock in the morning—four hours earlier than the original bus! The second bus arrived not long afterward and, with the elders on board, arrived in Brasília at six o'clock the next morning, hours before their originally scheduled bus arrived. This story showed me that yes, the Lord takes care of His servants when they are on His errand.

This next account was sent to me by Elder Newell, who had been in the mission field about six months, and it involves his companion, Elder Jacobson, a zone leader near the end of his mission. The experience shows how the zone leader was humble enough to follow promptings received by his junior companion.

Missed Bus?

"Two weeks ago Elder Jacobson and I were waiting for the bus at the bus stop. It was late, around nine o'clock at night. We were just talking about our day and everything that had happened when a thought entered my mind: 'Go to that street.' I thought, 'Okay,' so we went there, but nobody was out in the street. We started to knock on doors and we found a family that scheduled an appointment with us. Although I was happy about that, I was thinking that the family wasn't why we went there that night.

"This whole time we'd been listening for the sounds of an oncoming bus so we wouldn't miss it. We decided to go back to the bus stop, but alas, the bus had already passed and we could see it in the distance turning the corner. My companion jokingly said, 'Maybe you had a revelation to miss the bus.'

"So we waited for the next bus, which arrived fifteen minutes later. When we entered the bus, Elder Jacobson started to talk with a lady who was riding on the bus. This lady started to cry and said that she'd been having a lot of troubles with work and in her church. And also she had been praying to God, asking for help, and that He'd send His angels to help her. The thing that makes this story even cooler is this: she was waiting for the bus, the same bus that we missed, but it never passed. 'It always passes,' she said. And another thing—it turns out that she lives on that same street where I was told to go. We've been teaching her and things are going really well."

I can imagine how grateful the Lord was for the boldness of this missionary. I know that his example, and the other ones in this chapter, have inspired me to become more open to the Spirit's whisperings. How interesting it is that even rejecting a prompting can ultimately teach us to recognize the Lord's urgings.

Chapter 8

IN THE ZONE

And they were all filled with the Holy Ghost.

Acts 2:4

Sometimes the most powerful inspiration comes as we prepare to teach or help others in some way. I learned this lesson the hard way and ended up with an embarrassing story to teach the missionaries what not to do! The example is from an incident dated November 1, 2004, and recorded in my personal journal. I usually place a title at the top of my journal entries, and in this case, I dubbed the entry "A Thimble Full."

A Thimble Full

"A very interesting thing happened last night here at the hotel in Sinop, Mato Grosso. We had just finished participating in a regional conference with the Sinop and Sorriso branches and were preparing to go to Cuiabá to host a Zone Conference with the missionaries. Although we had already worked up a number of ideas to discuss at the conference, I was still concerned with some items. I felt that the new missionary program that was to be implemented, *Preach My Gospel*, would consume the majority of our conference time and that there wouldn't be enough time for some of the other things that I wanted to share.

"I went to sleep that night, but during an interval somewhere between sleep and awake, I was pondering on a number of conference alternatives. All of a sudden the Holy Ghost entered into my body with a force rarely experienced. I wondered if there was so much light radiating outward that anyone could easily see it. At that moment I became wide awake, but my body was very, very tired. The Spirit continued with me and I began to be given a huge amount of exciting information. It was like a vast inflow of ideas to my mind—ideas that were sublime and important to share.

"I got a prompting to arise and get a notebook so that I could register some of these ideas. I was hesitant for two reasons: first, I thought it might interrupt the inflow of ideas, and second, my body was so very tired. I thought that I would just concentrate and try to remember. I went over the thoughts one by one in my mind, repeating them in an effort to record them mentally. Again the thought came, 'get a notebook.' Once again, the flesh was weak and I felt that it would be better to try and remember them by repeating them in my mind. A third time the thought came, 'get a notebook!'

"Resignedly, I got up and shuffled around in search of a notebook. Not wanting to awaken my wife by turning on the light, I just went around in darkness looking for anything to write upon. Finally, I found a tiny, rectangular pad of hotel notepaper that was about 3 inches by 3½ inches. It may have had as many as three or four sheets remaining. I also located a hotel pen, so I went back to bed with these items in hand and said, 'Okay, Lord, I'm now ready.'

"What transpired next was that I could not get back in the spiritual state that I had been earlier. I strove my best to get back in that state, but it was fruitless. I then decided to write down what I had registered in my mind through repetition, but I was unable even to recall those phrases I had repeated to myself. Finally, I did remember just two words, so I wrote them on the small piece of paper . . . I waited for an inflow of more information, but none came.

"The next morning, when I awoke, I once again tried to get in tune so I could receive what the Lord had in store for me to share, but I got nothing. I looked over at the small piece of paper and saw the two words written on it: 'The book.' Thinking back on the context of the spiritual inflow of the previous night, I presumed that those two words were the Lord's way of telling me to concentrate on the book *Preach My Gospel* and not put such a high priority on the things that I personally had wanted to share with the missionaries.

"But I also learned a more important lesson. When the Lord is prepared to give you a bucket full of inspiration, it is inappropriate to go to him with merely a thimble. Indeed, it is insulting. I felt very bad about having done this—treating casually the onset of a divine inflow. I resolved to have a notebook at my bedside with a functioning pen the next night, but nothing came."

Four weeks later I added to this section of my journal a further comment:

"I have repeated this pattern each subsequent night for a month, but still nothing has come. I surmised that these experiences are so rare, we must always be prepared to receive them, else we may miss out of them, as I did on that occasion.

I can't remember the kind of information with which I was being flooded, and am sorry that the missionaries and I will be unable to benefit from it."

In retrospect, it is apparent to me (and disconcerting!) that I was neither thinking clearly nor acting in faith. First, I was prompted three times to get a notebook (which we had readily available in our luggage but would have required turning on a light). The first two times I thought that I knew better and would merely memorize as well as I could the messages that were being conveyed or reconstruct them later during the light of day. After all, I had confidence in my memorizing capabilities. I would show the Lord! The third time I finally acquiesced, yet rather than get a notebook, I instead got a single tiny pad of paper and pen—and this in the face of a flood of ongoing inspiration!

Second, why would I be fearful that if I obeyed the prompting from the Source of information, I would somehow remove myself from "the zone" of being attuned to that Source? Wouldn't He have the ability to renew the link? Yes, had I not doubted.

Third, worrying about awaking my wife by turning on the light might be a nice gesture under other circumstances, but when one receives a divine prompting, and no less than three times, wouldn't it be more reasonable to think that obedience is greater than chivalry? Indeed, when Moroni appeared to Joseph Smith three times during a single night, the room grew brighter than noon-day sun, yet none of Joseph's brothers who occupied that same small bedroom were stirred. I would have needed only to turn on a sixty-watt light bulb. Should I not have been more faithful to the promptings and left the details to our Maker? To put it succinctly, by my not switching on a small bulb, we all forfeited a veritable flood of light that would have blessed the entire mission. I have learned my lesson well. To this day, I sleep with a notebook and a pen by my bedside.

Divine Instructions

One of the missionaries set a better example. Elder Hunter (pseudonym) shared a marvelous experience with me during an interview, which I later recorded in my journal. He had recently attended a zone conference where we discussed the exercise of mighty prayer as we sought God's direction. He decided to engage in some mighty prayer himself, and then began reading the scriptures and meditating on them.

While he was doing this, Elder Hunter felt prompted to get paper and a pen and ready himself for instruction. He quickly complied and resumed his meditative posture. What followed was a veritable stream of information and instruction about his mission. He took it down as quickly and accurately as he was able, using several sheets of paper. He said that the stream turned into a flood.

Elder Hunter said that the instructions came in much the same form as a section of the Doctrine and Covenants. The inspiration contained detailed instructions and a vision of the future, a bit like a patriarchal blessing.

Elder Hunter's face brightened as he recounted this experience to me. His much-better example taught me the truth of the Prophet Joseph Smith's words: "the . . . Lord is ever ready to instruct such as diligently seek in faith" (*History of the Church,* 1:126).

Another admirable example comes from Elder Melendez, who sent this letter while he was serving as a branch president over the Posse, Goiás Branch. He was a very capable missionary, an elder who could be entrusted with the souls of those he served. I had every confidence that he would rely on the Lord to help him, rather than relying solely upon his own efforts.

Guidance through a Dream

"One Sunday night I arrived home from church and what made this Sunday different from all the others was the conversation I had with a member. This person had not come to church for a long time because of things that had happened to her.

"After our conversation I came home and knelt in my room to pray. I asked the Lord if He could please guide me as to what I should do and where I could find the information I needed. I had the church manuals and looked through them constantly but could not find the answer I was seeking. At the end of the day when we returned to our house I looked again and still could not find it. So I prayed and went to bed.

"That night I will never forget. As I slept, it felt as though someone came to me and they said that they were sent to get me. This person was dressed in pure white, so I followed him. He took me to a room that was pure white and then the room became brighter and brighter, I looked at the person who had brought me but I could not see his face; I just saw him point toward the source of light as if beckoning me to go ahead and ask. So I explained what was going on and that I was looking for some guidance as to what I should do. The light didn't say anything. All it did was extend its hand and point to the church manuals. I explained that I had looked and couldn't find what I was seeking. The hand then grabbed a piece of paper that had a number written on it. I took the number, and the person who brought me there took me by the hand and brought me back.

"As soon as I woke up I ran to my desk to find both books laid on my table. (The night before I had placed the books in my room on my bag.) I remembered the number and opened the book immediately. As I read the page it was exactly what I was seeking."

We can also see how important it is to pay attention to inspiration when we hear the other side of the story. The letters that follow were written by two sisters blessed by other missionaries' promptings and preparation.

Inspired Telephone Call

Sister Wetzel was serving in a town on the border of Bolivia, about eight hundred miles away from mission headquarters. She was training Sister Edson (pseudonym), a new missionary who had already decided that she wanted to go home. Sister Wetzel was desperately trying to convince this new missionary to stay, but she worried that her efforts were inadequate. The following comes from an entry on September 6 in Sister Wetzel's journal, used by permission.

"Sister Edson was insistent this morning that she cannot do this and wanted to go home. We prayed and talked, and I called Elder Chase, our zone leader, to say that we needed to talk to President. He said that he'd talk to President to tell him to call us. Sister Edson got in the shower while I made some treats for Regiano and Denise. The phone rang. I figured it was President. It was Elder Nunes, the assistant. He asked how things were. I said okay. He asked why it was just okay. I responded, 'Well, my companion wants to go home.' He said, 'Oh really? What's the problem?' I gave him a very brief rundown; I figured that Elder Chase had told him everything already. And then I said, 'Elder Chase talked to you, right?' He said, 'No, Sister.' He explained that he had just felt that he should call me and see how things were going. This is significant because I've met Elder Nunes only once, very briefly. He doesn't know me. But he said he felt he needed to call and tell me the Lord is pleased with our work. He continued, saying that during transfers, President had expressed a lot of confidence in me as a trainer, and Elder Nunes advised President to assign me to the missionary who most needed it. He said, 'There is not a sister in the mission [that is better suited than you] to help [this particular] companion. You have done your part. The Lord is pleased with that. He trusted you with one of His daughters and He is well pleased. You can have a peaceful heart.' Whoa.

"Here is the amazing thing. I've been worried about my companion, as has President, Elder Hadfield [the assistant overseeing and residing in the state of Mato Grosso], Elder Chase, and the whole branch. I haven't thought too much of me. But I've wondered about all of this, if this is my fault. I didn't even know how much I needed that phone call until I hung up, and it all hit me. Elder Nunes followed a prompting given by the Lord. The Lord spoke to me in my time of need through one of His servants. I can trust that. He is pleased with me and what I've done. As I realized all of this, I felt an overwhelming feeling of love and gratitude for my Heavenly Father. I knelt down right where I was in the kitchen, crying with gratitude, to thank Him. I know He lives and, as Elder [Neal A.] Maxwell says, 'God is in the details.' Of this I testify."

Elder Nunes called her without any prior communication from me. Spiritually attuned assistants like him made my job much easier. About six years after our missions had concluded, I traveled to southern Brazil and visited with Elder Nunes and his wife. I told him about Sister Wetzel's account and watched his eyes moisten as he learned how she treasured that timely phone call. I asked him if he recalled it, and he said that he did. I then asked if he had made other "random" calls to missionaries, and he said he didn't remember having made any others. I asked why he had decided to make that particular call, and he replied that he just felt that he should. He was one of many worthy missionaries who received divine guidance, though it hardly registered as a prompting at the time, and took action in a timely and inspired way.

The Lord Speaks through His Servants

Sister Pierce watched another missionary speak by the power of the Holy Ghost and wrote about it in a letter that touched me deeply.

"I had a sacred spiritual experience Sunday that I would like to share with you. We went with one of our investigators to the Asa Sul chapel for the special musical fireside of the restoration that the sisters organized. Overall, it was a great fireside. In between musical numbers, Elder Harbuck spoke about dispensations, Christ's earthly ministry and Joseph Smith. While he was up on stage, halfway through his talk, I was enveloped in what he was saying—the energy and power and spirit with which he spoke. Then I noticed a light around his whole body. I tried to focus my eyes to get rid of the light. I rubbed them but the light stayed around him. As he continued to bear powerful witness the thought—the voice—it wasn't just a thought—and it wasn't my own voice—came to me. 'This is not Elder Harbuck speaking, this is Heavenly Father through the Holy Ghost speaking directly through Elder Harbuck.' The power and authority with which he spoke were not his own. I was awestruck—my mind and body seemed to be in a different place for an instant.

"Then on Monday I read *On Wings of Faith.*[10] One of the experiences talked about 'spiritual eyes.' I don't know if I've ever really thought about this concept.

10 *On Wings of Faith* is a book written by my father, Frederick W. Babbel, about his experiences with Ezra Taft Benson in Europe after World War II. I received permission to share the book with the missionaries.

But I believe what I saw Sunday night at the fireside was with spiritual eyes. I am so grateful to my Heavenly Father for this experience and the witness of the power of God, and the knowledge that He really does speak through us."

The final story gives an example of an elder who sought inspiration to answer a dilemma. He was preparing a discussion for a man named Rogério when he encountered a scripture that puzzled him. This elder's diligent attempt to find an answer to his own question led to a distinct spiritual experience, which he recorded for me shortly after his mission.

Like a Butterfly Resting on a Tree

"We were planning to go into depth about Joseph Smith and the Restoration, and I was preparing for in-depth questions about the authority of the priesthood. I cross-referenced into D&C 84:19–21, and the following sequence of phrases caught my attention: 'without . . . the authority of the priesthood . . . no man can see the face of God, even the Father, and live.'

"I saw this scripture and panicked as I immediately thought of the First Vision. I couldn't understand in my limited mind how this doctrine could be true while at the same time Joseph could see God the Father and Jesus Christ as a fourteen-year-old boy. I was distraught. As time went on and my search to understand didn't bring any apparent fruition to me, my anxiety heightened. I didn't know what to do, or where to turn. I was an assistant to the president and training one of the best missionaries in the mission, and was about to teach someone who would certainly have pointed questions for us. All I could do was pray.

"I knelt down at the foot of the bed with my missionary companion, and poured out my heart honestly and humbly (I couldn't figure this problem out on my own) to Heavenly Father. I was distraught because all I knew to be true seemed, if only for a moment, to be completely under attack and upside down, and I couldn't see the end from the beginning.

"We prayed earnestly, and after a very short time, my consciousness of the current situation froze and I was no longer in Gama, but was in a forest, watching a boy. What I saw must have only been a few moments long, but it will forever be emblazoned upon my mind. The boy was kneeling, facing diagonally away from me, and then light filled the forest. It started from the canopy, then came downward in a shaft, at the same time that it swept outwards. It expanded until it filled my view of the whole forest. It was a warm, bright feeling.

"The vision ended very soon after it started, but it seemed to me that time froze and I literally felt like I was there, almost like a butterfly resting on a tree, watching the scene unfold.

"I got up off of my knees, having been filled with the Spirit of the Lord, and knowing that even though I didn't understand the scripture very well, I knew that Joseph Smith saw both God the Father and Jesus Christ in the grove of trees that morning. I learned that morning that my mind was finite and incapable of understanding everything there was to know at the moment, but that I should trust the Lord and go forward in faith, trusting that later on, all things would be revealed.

"Since then, I have found several ways of understanding this scripture, and thankfully have been able to synthesize and understand what was an apparent paradox to me at the time."

I find it interesting that this elder's spiritual experience didn't answer his exact question, but that it gave him the keys necessary for him ultimately to obtain the understanding he desired. It is marvelous how our Heavenly Father responds to earnest prayers!

Chapter 9

"IN THE VERY HOUR"

For it shall be given you in the very hour, yea, in the very moment, what ye shall say.

D&C 100:6

Ideally, a missionary would prepare to teach by customizing each lesson ahead of time through study and inspiration. In our mission, with no cars for the missionaries and only one cell phone per sprawling zone, much of a missionary's day after morning individual and companionship study was spent in going to and from appointments that may or may not pan out and meeting with new people on the streets and buses. It was not possible to prepare for every teaching situation and scenario. Thankfully, the Lord provided a way around this problem. He told Joseph Smith and Sidney Rigdon:

Lift up your voices to this people, speak the thoughts that I shall put into your hearts, and you shall not be confounded before men;

For it shall be given you in the very hour, yea, in the very moment, what ye should say. (D&C 100:5–6)

The missionaries saw this promise fulfilled frequently. It wasn't always easy for them to listen to the whisperings of the Spirit while they were teaching, but when they did pay heed, they taught with boldness. They sensed that they were being guided by a power higher than their own. It was wonderful to hear from missionaries who were able to communicate things the Spirit prompted them to say "in the very hour."

Inspired to Make a List

Sister Ward and her companion, Sister Brewer, were teaching a woman named Carmen, who readily accepted the gospel message and even started attending church, but just couldn't cut the habit of drinking.

Sister Ward wrote, "One night, about 10 days ago, we were talking to her once again and just trying to figure out what to say or what we could do to help her break this habit. During that conversation, something came to my mind—to tell her to write down ten reasons why she shouldn't drink every time she felt the desire. I thought about it for a minute and translated the words in my head, and at first I thought, 'I don't know if I should say it, because it is not a normal thing we'd do and I'm so new here to the mission and don't know how all these things work.' Then I thought, 'But the thought came to my mind; I have to say it.' And right as I started to talk, the Spirit just filled the room as I explained this idea. It testified to me that it was inspiration that she needed.

"The Spirit was so strong that in the days that followed, I wanted to know how she was doing with it and to see if it changed her, because I really felt that it would . . . When we got back [from a zone conference in Cuiabá], we visited her and she had only drunk one time in a week! And now she's preparing to be baptized and is so excited. She hasn't drunk anything ever since!"

"You Must Make a Very Important Decision!"

In his weekly letter, Elder Evilasio wrote about a woman who faced a different obstacle to her conversion. Although I don't know the ending to this story, I love reading about times when these missionaries were given the words they needed to say. His story comes from a discussion he had with the woman and her family.

"The Spirit of the Lord came very strongly and said: 'Tell her that she must make a very important decision. The reason that she has not been baptized yet is because she works on the Sabbath day.' The Spirit's message that she needed to leave her job and be baptized was very clear to me. The problem with this solution, I thought, was that she was the only one who worked in that house. I could not tell her to leave her job! All of a sudden, after much internal debate, I remembered that I needed to speak that very instant. I bowed my head as I thought how I could say those things. Suddenly, I saw something that I could not explain. There was a light coming from behind me that was so strong, that I raised my head. All perceived the light as I mustered enough strength to say: 'You must make a very important decision!'

"All were surprised and the mother of the young woman said, 'God just spoke with him.' I knew that the Lord was using me as his mouthpiece to tell that young woman what she needed to do. I stayed quiet for a few moments, and when my companion was reading a scripture, the Spirit came to me with that same power and made my heart beat rapidly.

"Then I began to say many things, although I do not remember all of what I said. I do remember saying: 'You need to be baptized. Heavenly Father is so happy that you have accepted His truths. He loves you so much, Célia, and He has a great work to be done through you. He will not leave you alone, nor abandoned . . .' When I returned to my normal self, I looked at Célia and her face was moistened with abundant tears. She understood the decision that she needed to make and told us she would report her decision to us within the week."

Listening to Cues

For many of the missionaries, the ability to reach an investigator came when they felt inspired to share scriptures or other gospel resources. Elder Lavelli reported one such instance about a time when he was teaching a new investigator and felt inspired to share something he had never used before.

"While there," he wrote, "a friend of our investigator arrived and stayed to hear the message and something very different happened to me. When my companion [Elder Fernandes] began, I perceived that he would speak about Joseph Smith and the restoration and I was guided by the Spirit to read verses 8, 10 and 11 from the Joseph Smith History, but I fought against that idea because until that moment in my mission, I had never taught by reading those passages. But when I commenced to speak about the prophet, I began to read and explain as if I had already studied a lot about that at home. Then I perceived that the friend of the investigator began to be very attentive, and I related the vision in my words and had an assuredness that the Spirit had touched that woman.

"When the lesson ended, I invited the visitor to hear the messages in her house by saying, 'I would like to invite . . .' but she cut me off and said 'yes!' I then asked her, 'Yes, what? I hadn't even finished my invitation!' She responded, 'I felt in my bosom that you were going to invite me to hear the lessons in my house, and the answer is yes, I accept!'"

He continued, "This is marvelous! I love this work and my Savior and know how important it is to hear the whisperings of the Spirit."

Emboldened by the Spirit

This final account comes from the weekly report of an elder who was quiet by nature, but who was able to act boldly as he was led by the Holy Ghost.

"Yesterday we were at the home of an investigator, Adriana," Elder Schultz wrote. "She has depression due to gossip about her in the workplace. She has a daughter of nine years of age, and they live together in an apartment.

"We began to give a follow-up message about the Book of Mormon. (She had still not prayed to know of its truthfulness.) I asked her why she had neither read nor prayed about it, and then I bore my testimony to her. This brought a spirit so strong that I began to feel something different. I didn't exactly know what it was. All of a sudden, words began to spring forth from my mouth and I said: 'You have to spend more time with your daughter and you must teach her to follow the correct path.' I marveled at what I had said and Adriana replied: 'I know that it is God who is speaking this to me.' The Spirit touched her very strongly. She said she will begin praying, and I know that she will be baptized.

"I am so happy that I feel like another person. I learned the value of work and I will work with more vigor until the end. I thank God very much for being here. I now feel prepared for anything."

In the end, the decision to change lies with the investigator. Still, the benefits of heeding the promptings of the Spirit didn't begin and end with those that they taught. Elder Schultz's reaction, "I am so happy that I feel like another person," shows the Spirit's renewing effect on each one of these elders and sisters as they allowed themselves to become true messengers of the Lord.

The last sentence of Elder Schultz's letter about now feeling prepared for anything was soon put to the test. Shortly after I received this letter, Elder Schultz was feeling very sick. He had his lungs examined at a hospital, but the doctors found nothing wrong. I was about 600 miles away from where he was working in Palmas when I received his call. Despite the Palmas doctors' diagnosis (or lack thereof), I somehow perceived that this was a potentially serious enough medical emergency that I should send Elder Schultz home immediately to Curitiba, some 1300 miles distant. I sensed that he should *not* take the next scheduled bus to Brasília (which would not arrive to its destination until almost twenty-two hours later) and then fly to Curitiba after meeting with me. Instead, I felt that he should catch the first available plane from Palmas directly to Curitiba. Such a decision was costly and unprecedented for me, and I was saddened that I wouldn't even get a chance to say goodbye to Elder Schultz in person.

When Elder Schultz arrived that night at the Curitiba airport, his parents met him there and over his protest, wisely decided to take him to the hospital immediately. The doctors in Curitiba found that one of Elder Schultz's lungs had been punctured and was now collapsed. The worse news was that the other lung was also almost collapsed because the blood from the punctured lung had filled his entire chest cavity with fluid and was leaving no room for the good lung to fill with air. He was told that he was extremely fortunate to have arrived at that hour, because had he waited another couple of hours, he would have died.

Chapter 10

THE ELECT

And ye are called to bring to pass the gathering of mine elect; for mine elect hear my voice and harden not their hearts.

D&C 29:7

The Lord defined the elect as those who "hear my voice and harden not their hearts" (D&C 29:7). Some of the elect are quick to accept the gospel and others take their time, but the hearts of each eventually embrace the gospel message. I read with joy many accounts from missionaries who were led to find these individuals, and this chapter contains examples that I found especially striking. Each story reminds me of what's at stake when we do missionary work—the reason the Lord charged us to gather his elect, oftentimes far from the comforts of home. As Ammon said, "If we had not come up out of the land of Zarahemla, these our dearly beloved brethren . . . would also have been strangers to God" (Alma 26:9). Each of the following examples shows the urgency of missionary work.

Prepared by a Dream

When Elder Caine and his companion began teaching Eva, a young woman who ran her own event-planning company, they seemed familiar to her, but not because of any previous acquaintance. Not long after their first meeting, she told the elders about the dream she had had before she met them.

Elder Caine wrote, "In this dream she said she saw two men, dressed like us, who walked up to her." He continued, "She said she couldn't see one, but the other looked exactly like me. She said that he gave her a piece of paper and told her to read it and then left. Then she woke up and told everyone about it.

"The next day [after the dream], while we were passing by her house, she saw us and asked if I was teaching English. I said yes. She asked if she could come to the class. I told her she could. Then she came and after English class she asked if we would teach her about our church. We taught her that very day and in the first discussion we made a timeline from Adam and Eve to our days in 2004. I made it to help her understand better and to study. But she told us that in her dream, that piece of paper she got was identical to the timeline we gave her. The Spirit was strong at that moment and for another reason I was shown one of the many ways the Lord prepares His children to hear His gospel. She then asked about baptism and we explained it. She didn't accept yet, but I'm sure she will someday."

Eva was baptized five weeks later, on June 27, into the Planalto Ward of the North Brasília Stake.

Investigator Dreams

The following account, from Sister Luzia Ivani de Almeida and Sister Luciane Santos da Conceição, tells the story of a man prepared eight years ahead of time to receive help from these two sister missionaries. They were teaching a different investigator when this man came along and decided that he, too, wanted to listen.

"When we were speaking at the beginning of our discussion about the apostasy, the gentleman made a comment that was very interesting.

"He said that about eight years ago, he suffered an accident and stayed for a few months in a hospital while he was in a coma or unconscious. During that time he had a dream or something similar. He related that during this dream a nurse came close to him and said that two women would arrive to help him. One of the women was named Luzia and the other Lucia. But as he found out later, after coming out of his coma, there was no one with these names who worked in the hospital. The man was left understanding nothing.

"What is most interesting is that he said these women would speak to him of Jesus Christ. Finally, President, what I was getting to was what Sister Almeida and I are named: Luzia and Luciane. He said one of our names exactly, and the other one almost exactly. There is no way this man could have known our first names, as they do not appear on our nametags, and he had just met us. I know only that the Spirit was very strong and this man is very special."

Names on a Piece of Paper

From Elder Quêvedo I received a weekly missionary letter that intrigued me enough that I did some follow-up research with his former companion.

"When I was with Elder Ballard in Várzea Grande, Mato Grosso, one night a child came to speak with me in a dream, and spoke five names to me—two names of men and three of females. In the dream I saw the face of each person and noted their names on a piece of paper. The dream awakened me, so immediately I remembered and wrote down four of these names on a piece of paper. I remembered the fifth person only by her appearance. In the two cases relating to men, I was also given information about where they resided. The next day, I mentioned this experience to my companion and showed to him the four names that I had noted on the piece of paper in my dream. We didn't know what to think of that experience and had never before met these people whose names I related to my companion."

A few months after the fact, I talked on the phone with Elder Ballard (Elder Quêvedo's companion at the time of the dream) to investigate what happened next. He could still remember the names that Elder Quêvedo had spoken to him: José, Pedro, Jéssica, and Bruna. The fifth person was just a face. Elder Quêvedo had described to him in great detail what each person looked like and what their approximate ages were. He could give information about the neighborhoods that the two men lived in, and in José's case, he could even name the street, just from the memory of the dream.

Elder Ballard remarked that once he learned of these names, he felt that they needed to find these people right away. He and Elder Quêvedo spent their entire Preparation Day making contacts. They walked all over, talking with anybody they saw. After several hours of work and no investigator to show for it, Elder Ballard was fatigued. Elder Quêvedo told him, "Maybe I had this dream because it was the only way the Lord could get you to make more contacts!"

Later that evening the elders rode a bus toward an unfamiliar neighborhood on a mission to find José. They stepped off at the first bus stop in that neighborhood and started looking for 9th Street, the street that Elder Quêvedo recalled from the dream. There were no visible road signs. The elders felt impressed to ask a woman on the street where 9th Street was located. She told them that 9th Street was where she was headed, and she asked them whom they sought. When they told her they were looking for José, she replied that there was only one José she knew of on that street and that he was her husband. She invited the elders to follow her to her home, where they met José.

The elders began to teach the lessons to him and later found someone named Pedro who accepted the discussions as well. By the time of my call to

Elder Ballard, one had already been baptized and the other was still receiving the discussions.

As for the women named in the dream, Elder Quêvedo had a harder time finding them. Even after spending several days looking for these women, the elders never came up with any leads on them. It wasn't until Elder Quêvedo moved to a new area that he found them. He wrote the following in a letter:

"Yesterday, two months after having had that dream, and having since been transferred to labor in a small city about 1,000 kilometers to the east of the place where I had been working with Elder Ballard, my new companion. Elder Gonçalves and I, along with a local member named Moisés, baptized 3 people. Two of them had the same names of those whom I had noted on the piece of paper in my dreams two months earlier in Várzea Grande. I baptized Jéssica and her name was on that piece of paper. My companion baptized Bruna, whose name was also on that piece of paper. Moisés baptized a woman named Priscila, and although her name was not on that piece of paper, I recognized her face, for I had seen it in that same dream."

When I related this information about Jéssica, Bruna, and Priscila's baptism to Elder Ballard, he—well, he could hardly believe it!

Elder Quêvedo was one of many missionaries who recognized certain people or had precognitive experiences about people to contact in their next city—before receiving word about a transfer. It is sobering to realize how crucial it is in some cases that I get the transfer assignments "right"—if I had simply acted on my own, these five people may have not come to know the gospel.

Praying for an Elect Family

From Elder Pickett I received the following letter, and later a follow-up email.

"On the long bus from Cáceres to Brasília the bus driver started swerving and going all over the road. I was sitting in the front seat above the driver on the double decker bus, and it kind of made me nervous. I started to pray for comfort. The [second segment of the] bus ride was around twenty hours so I decided to pray for a while. I thanked Heavenly Father for my mission up to that point and reviewed many blessings I had received. After a very long time praying, I felt to ask that the Lord provide a whole family that I could teach and be baptized. I have worked with many families and baptized many people, but I really want to experience being a part of converting a whole family. I have hoped and prayed for a chance to be a part of converting a family ever since meeting with Washington's family back in Rondonópolis with Elder Priest. I asked with much faith and again expressed that I have worked very hard and would love to have this blessing.

"I finished the prayer after a few more thoughts and went to sleep.

"When I arrived in Brasília I met my new companion, Elder Handley. The first thing he said to me was, 'Elder Pickett you are so lucky, WE JUST FOUND A GOLDEN FAMILY TO TEACH!!!'

Elder Pickett was thrilled to have his prayer answered. Eleven years later, Elder Pickett gave me an update on that family. He reported: "That family was baptized, sealed [in the temple] and now one of their two daughters has been sealed to a faithful [returned] missionary! What a blessing to be present for someone's baptism, confirmation, endowment, and sealing! Just two days ago I received an email from one of the daughters," Elder Pickett continued. "She reminded me that April 10th [2015] was their 11-year anniversary as members of the church! To celebrate she was going to the temple! They are truly an elect family."

Dream about an Investigator

Elder Gonçalves wrote: "This week I had a wonderful experience. On Monday night or Tuesday early morning, I had a dream in which I was delivering a lantern to a blonde-haired woman. She took it in her hand and began to cry and thank me. She said, 'Thank you very much for having brought the light into our home.'

"After a missionary conference on Friday, August 13th, we received a referral. We went to seek out this referral, which we had received on a friendship card. When we arrived there, we met two families that were very special. We imparted to them the gospel principles associated with the fourth discussion. What was most interesting was that the woman I dreamed about earlier in the week, to whom I had delivered a lantern, was the same woman in one of these two families! She was the director of education at a high school.

"Her family consisted of six people: herself, her husband, their children, and a son-in-law. I know that the Lord's hand is in this work, and that if we put forth our best efforts, we will see these miracles. She was unable to receive our message at that time because she was going to travel to have surgery due to smoking.

"Upon the completion of her surgery, she returned to Brazlândia and we taught her. I was transferred away from that city at the end of September and so I telephoned her prior to leaving, and over the telephone she said: 'Thank you very much for having brought the light into our home.'"

Vision during a Lesson

Sometimes the elect come in curious packages, with a set of daunting challenges. Elder Ricardo learned this at the beginning of his mission. He had been sent by the previous mission president on an emergency transfer in a last-ditch effort to help salvage the mission of an elder—one who was approaching the end of a disheartening two years. Elder Ricardo was issued this assignment even though he was relatively new on his mission at that time. Below is taken from his journal.

"Arriving [at my new location], I met the elder in a stage of rather deep despair. His discouragement was such that on that day he hardly spoke a word to me. That night he would not participate with me in planning our work for next day. My attempts to engage him in the planning were simply ignored.

"I felt very sorrowful and rather helpless, and sensed a need to pray. I waited for him to go to sleep (around midnight), and retired to our backyard where we had a mango tree. Underneath that tree I prayed to Heavenly Father for about an hour and a half expressing my distress and asking Him fervently to help me because I simply did not know what to do in this situation.

"The next morning I woke up and did my gospel study alone because my companion was still asleep. After studying, while ironing my shirt next to the window . . . I had a feeling of joy in my heart that was gradually filling my soul until, all of a sudden, the Spirit spoke very clearly in my mind: 'Today, two people will accept baptism!'

"Moved by this wonderful feeling from what the Spirit had just confirmed to me, I called to my companion excitedly and said: 'Elder, today two people will accept baptism!' He shifted on the bed and replied, with an air of disbelief, 'Yeah, right. Sure.' He knew that over the previous eight months the missionaries had knocked on the door of every house in the proselyting area without any success.

"When we left our home to begin work, he told me, somewhat sarcastically, 'Elder, since you are so full of faith, what we do today is up to you!'

"This really worried me as I was new to the mission and new to the area, but I took the challenge and believed. I looked left, then right and said, 'Let's start by heading to the left.'

"I felt impressed that we begin by knocking on a particular door, the door of the house next to ours. A neighbor who lived there, a nice lady of about 40 or 50 years of age, peeked through the curtain of the window and closed it quickly. My companion, who had warned me that she would do that, since she had done the same thing a few times before with other missionaries, taunted me, 'Ha ha! I told you so!' Nonetheless, I remained in front of the house without reacting to his taunting. Then she opened the curtain again and motioned for us to enter. I smiled and glanced over at my dumbfounded companion as he pretended not to react. We went in and I had to teach the lesson alone . . .

"During that era of the mission, the second lesson was usually the one where we typically challenged the investigators to agree to be baptized if and when they reached a conviction that our message was true. However, I felt that particular day that we should present a combined first and second lesson and then issue the baptismal challenge. So I did. She readily accepted baptism. We set a target date and then left.

"My companion was reluctant to accept that something wonderful was happening and said that her acceptance of the commitment that day was just a coincidence."

As the end of the day neared, Elder Ricardo and his companion still had not met anybody else who was interested in hearing their message, much less accepting a baptismal commitment. On their way back home, for some reason the senior companion said they might as well stop by a struggling investigator's house. It was a house where three generations of family lived under one roof, but the only investigator was a young woman in her twenties who had not progressed very well. When they arrived, she greeted them adorned with nose and navel jewels, several layers of earrings, and various body piercings. She wore a skimpy T-shirt with the emblem of a heavy metal band known for its lewdness. Her mother, the matriarch of the three generations, was in the adjoining room ironing some clothes.

There was heaviness about this young woman's spirit, but she invited the elders in and allowed them to present a message. She slumped back onto the sofa and seemed rather disconnected to the message as they delivered it.

Elder Ricardo and his companion took turns in presenting to her the principles contained in the missionary lesson. During the first principle, Elder Ricardo was burdened by a very troubling, ominous feeling, but he continued to teach until his principle had been presented and he then turned the lesson over to his senior companion. In the middle of delivering the next principle, the senior companion stopped suddenly, hesitated for a few seconds, and then continued. At that same moment, the Holy Spirit spoke to Elder Ricardo and impelled him to stand up, interrupt, and say with urgency the following: "Do not do tomorrow what you are planning on doing!" Elder Ricardo opened his mouth and spoke as directed. He was shocked at his own boldness, as was the investigator.

"My senior companion then stood up and confirmed my warning, saying, 'I also felt impressed that I should say the exact same thing.' (In a later conversation with my companion, he told me that at the very moment when he had earlier paused while teaching the gospel principle, he had received the same prompting that I did, but didn't have the courage to speak up.)"

The young woman moved to the front edge of the sofa, shocked and troubled that Elder Ricardo knew something about her plans for the next day. Her mother, who had been silent up to that point, stopped her ironing and in loud voice and an air of indignation asked her daughter, "What are you going to do tomorrow?" Her daughter then asked Elder Ricardo what he knew about it.

At that very moment, Elder Ricardo saw a vision of the young woman gathering two young children together, hugging them and saying goodbye to each of them. He said, "In this brief glimpse, I saw her lean down and speak to the little boy and girl, who were facing her but had their backs to me. I sensed a horrible dark, and deeply sad feeling and knew that she was about to abandon them and step into a very perilous situation. I felt the urgency of her situation and told her what I saw, and she broke down crying, admitting that she had reached a point beyond any hope, and had planned on doing that very thing the next morning.

"She told me that the two young children were hers, who at that time were playing in a bedroom in the house. Up to that moment, I knew nothing about her having any children as it was the first time I had met her and my companion had said nothing about them. I then implored her not to go through with her plan, that God was very concerned about her, loved her, and that she *must not* do that! The young woman appeared to marvel that God would even care about her.

"She then explained to us her predicament. She revealed that she was involved with drugs. (I didn't ask her if she was a user, seller, or both.) She had run up a heavy debt to her drug suppliers that she could never repay. She had delayed to make payment several times and angered her suppliers. They gave her one more day to pay in full and she expressed that they threatened to do something really bad to her and her entire family if she did not pay the debt, implying that there would be deaths, to teach her a lesson and make of her an example for their other clients. Their threats filled her with terror. Not being able to repay her debt, she felt that the only way she could protect her family was to travel to her suppliers' town some distance away, let them know that she had no funds, and face certain death herself. She figured that with her dead, the drug suppliers would not take any further action against her family. It was her only hope to save them."

Upon hearing this confession, her mother became very upset with her daughter and entered the living room. She apparently did not know that her daughter was involved with drugs. She spoke angrily to her daughter who had now placed their entire family in jeopardy because of it.

At this point the senior companion abruptly stood up and felt impressed to speak boldly to the young woman. He said, "I promise you in the name of Jesus Christ that if you agree to follow Christ and enter into baptism, you will be protected and the drug suppliers will not enter this town and cause harm to your family."

Elder Ricardo, who was still standing, reported, "I next felt impelled to witness to her that my companion's promise was inspired because I too was prompted to make her the same promise. A tense silence fell over the group. The young woman then got off the sofa and fell upon her knees, overcome with joy and hope. She hugged our legs and committed not to go through with her plans, but instead to receive other missionary lessons and then be baptized. We were taken aback at her display and told her not to embrace our legs, but to thank her Father in Heaven, who was making that promise to her through us. Her mother was amazed and overcome with her daughter's abrupt turnaround, and at our warnings and the powerful Spirit accompanying the promise."

The story then takes a very surprising turn. A couple of days later, after not receiving the promised payment, the three drug lords who had been supplying the young woman drove toward her town, ostensibly to take action against the family. As was reported in the newspaper the next day, they came with their guns. As they reached the outskirts of the town, the drug lords unexpectedly came upon a heavily armed military police blitz. (These blitzes were undertaken from time to time where each car would be stopped and identifying documents checked.) This blitz was positioned to surprise the people as they came upon it suddenly so they could not turn their cars around to avoid them, but must wait in line to speak with the police. Upon entering the unforeseen police blitz, the drug lords had to go slowly, in a single open lane of traffic, until they reached the officers and it was their turn to show their documents. The military police signaled for them to pull over but the drug lords instead sped away in their car toward the town. The police then leveled their rifles at the car and began shooting. The drug lords shot back and a firefight ensued. Two of the drug lords were killed and the third one escaped and fled from the town.

Later that month, after receiving all of the missionary lessons and keeping the commitments given to her, the young woman was baptized. Elder Ricardo's inspiration on his first morning in Cuiaba—that they would meet two people on that day who would commit to be baptized—was fulfilled. And their inspired promise to the young woman proved true, as her pursuers had not been able to enter the town and the lone survivor never returned.

Not long thereafter, Elder Ricardo reported that all members of the household who were of age were baptized into the LDS church, including the matriarch and patriarch of the three generations and the teenage brothers of the young woman.

But something even more remarkable happened. Prior to her baptism, the matriarch was so impressed with what had happened that she went from house to house throughout the neighboring area and related to each family what had happened. Because she was such a well-respected and trusted woman and a leading member of her congregation, her report piqued their interest. Soon, several of them began to attend the LDS ward. Within two months, there was a group of more than 60 of them joining with her family each Sunday as they all walked to church together. The chapel was filled with investigators! About half of them were soon baptized. Elder Ricardo was then transferred but heard that several others in that group later were baptized. (Within three years, both of the teenage brothers were called to serve missions in Elder Ricardo's hometown mission, where he got to see them serve. Their father served as elders quorum president.)

This experience was a watershed experience for the senior companion and helped him finish his mission with more conviction about its worth. That companion gained some confidence because although he had refused to act on his first prompting, leaving it to his junior companion to issue the warning, he had learned to trust his prompting because his junior companion had the exact same one. This helped him gain sufficient courage to stand up and make that bold promise to the young woman when he received his next prompting.

To me, it showed once again how God looks after all of His children—in this case, the young woman investigating the Church as well as the senior companion. Elder Ricardo learned the Lord's elect do not always come "packaged" in the same way. The woman they taught that first morning looked prepared for the gospel, while the younger woman, with her dress, jewelry, piercings, and lifestyle, appeared to be heading in a different direction. Nonetheless, she demonstrated nobility by being willing to sacrifice her own life to protect the lives of her entire family. She also demonstrated great faith in the inspired promises of the elders.

Truly, the Good Shepherd knows His sheep (John 10:14). What a privilege it is for us to help find them.

Chapter 11

THE MISSION CD

For my soul delighteth in the song of the heart; yea, the song of the righteous is a prayer unto me, and it shall be answered with a blessing upon their heads.

D&C 25:12

One of the most important things that happened on our mission began as a whim, almost an accident. The fruits of this idea spread so far that later, we'd look back and see it as one of the principal reasons that we—and especially my wife—were called to serve.

It started with a phone call. Sister Weller, an award-winning professionally trained vocalist, called to say that she had seen a small recording studio in her proselyting area. She asked whether my wife would be willing to accompany her for a few hours on the following Preparation Day to record songs for her investigators and friends. Mary Jane, musical devotee that she is, readily agreed. But as the two of them planned the recordings, the idea grew bigger—why not involve more voices in the effort? For that matter, why not produce a mission CD with a variety of solos, ensembles, and choruses?

By the end of the day, the idea had taken root both in their minds and in mine. Mary Jane and I had often lamented the absence of professionally recorded LDS music in Portuguese. Even though we had never seriously considered filling this hole before, it started to make almost too much sense as we pondered the possibilities. We had a large number of extraordinary singers in our mission—a statistical anomaly that had often seemed curious to us. My wife, a well-trained musician who had led choirs and performed, arranged, and accompanied music for decades, was the perfect candidate to spearhead such a project. We started to see the idea of a high-quality musical recording as something unique that our mission could offer to Brazil.

Before we could move ahead with the idea, we had to clear some hurdles. The first was location. How many of our talented singers could actually commute to the studio to record music? The geography of our mission extended (measured in driving distance) about 1,000 miles, west to east, and well over 700 miles, north to south. Mary Jane asked to see the map of companionship assignments in order to determine whether a critical mass of singers existed near the studio's location in Brasília. What she saw surprised her. Twenty-one of the mission's best vocalists, including some who had sung professionally, were currently working in the Distrito Federal, within easy distance of the studio. What serendipity (or, as it turned out, divine providence) that was. Never before or since did we have such a concentration of talented vocalists in one place at the same time.

The concentration wouldn't last, though, which brought us to our next issue: timing. Only three weeks remained until transfers, when four of our best vocalists would return home (including the sister who had found the studio), and others would be transferred many hundreds of miles away from Brasília. We had to act fast if we wanted to make this CD. We quickly chose the music and began rehearsals.

Another problem became apparent the minute we walked into the studio for the first time. The space was far too small. It was a studio designed for a solo guitar or small rock and roll band, not large choral numbers. There weren't nearly enough jacks or headphones to help the singers hear the accompaniment, so recording any larger choruses would be very problematic and require a lot of sound editing. One of the elders serving as financial clerk in the mission office at the time happened to be a recording artist who had experience using sound-mixing technology. This missionary, Elder Osmond, was undaunted by the situation and happy to help, so we designated him as our sound engineer. It felt almost too perfect to be true. We were able to move ahead with confidence.

We spent a few Preparation Days recording and re-recording the music in many phases. The skills that our sound engineer brought to the project cannot be overstated. He painstakingly edited each track of each recording, including a keyboard track, first sopranos track, second sopranos track, altos, and so on. In one case, he coordinated eighty-four tracks on a single song! With his help, not only did the studio's size become a non-issue, the entire CD became a polished production.

We initially commissioned five thousand copies of the CD for manufacture, which were quickly given away for free to investigators and members. Another three thousand copies followed soon thereafter. (No mission or church funds were expended for paying royalties to the composers/arrangers or in the recording, glass mastering, or manufacture of the CDs. Also, no attributions to our mission or the performing musicians were included in the CD insert or cover. This was done in response to suggestions from our mission overseers, who generally wouldn't condone such a project and did not want to encourage other missions to follow suit, but were willing to make an exception for our mission because of its unusual assemblage of musical talent.)

Elder Osmond and studio aide mixing the various song tracks

It didn't take long to see the effects of this project. Missionaries would walk down the streets and hear the music echoing from the windows of member homes, sometimes even nonmember homes. Ward and stake choirs began to learn and perform the beautiful arrangements. We started hearing the music in restaurants and even on radio stations. As missionaries returned home or sent copies of the CD to their families, the music began to spread all over Brazil. One thing became clear: the Saints had been starving for such music. The locals made untold copies of the songs and within a short time, many tens of thousands had heard the music recorded on that CD.

One of the most talented musicians in our mission was Elder Nielsen. An exceptional singer with professional experience, Elder Nielsen, at the time, was laboring some five hundred miles away from Brasília. A worse problem was that due to visa problems, Elder Nielsen had to leave Brazil within three weeks. Arrangements had been made for him to finish his mission in the United States. Even though we had twenty-one excellent singers close to the area of the studio,

I thought we needed this particular elder's help in order to make a good CD, so I asked him to stay in Brasília after a zone leader's conference and work with a different companion for the remaining weeks of his mission. He was the only elder transferred from afar to participate in the recording project.

Sister Weller, Elder Nielsen, Sister VanKatwyk, and Elder Osmond recording "If With All Your Heart" by Felix Mendelssohn

After the missionaries recorded the music, Elder Nielsen told me about a promise he had received in the blessing he was given when set apart for his mission. The promise was that tens of thousands of the Brazilian people would hear his voice in song. Yet as Elder Nielsen approached his final days in Brazil, this promise had gone unfulfilled. He had performed occasionally before a couple of small congregations of the Church and at mission zone conferences, but certainly not before more than a few hundred people. We were completely unaware of this promise when we invited him to participate in the mission CD project. Elder Nielsen left Brazil to finish his mission in the United States just a couple of days after making exquisite recordings of solos, duets, and mixed quartets—music destined to be heard and appreciated by tens of thousands of people in Brazil, and fulfilling a divine promise.

Our goal in making the mission CD was to uplift and inspire listeners. To our astonishment, the CD also became the catalyst for many faith-filled stories.

Elders Knighton, Middleton, Nielsen, Williams, and Osmond recording—note the inadequate number of earphones.

The Temperamental CD Player

The first story came from Elder Forrest and Elder Duncan, who sent me separate letters about this incident, which have been synthesized into one narrative here.

Elder Forrest and Elder Duncan had been asked to visit a family of inactive members. They scheduled a family home evening and planned to give a copy of the CD to the family during the visit. The husband, an influential politician and an inactive returned missionary, was still away when the elders arrived. Instead of starting the family home evening without him, the elders decided to help the mother clean the living room area and kitchen from the mess the kids had left, so that when her husband returned, that section of the house would be a clean, uplifting environment for family home evening.

Even after the missionaries cleaned the rooms, the husband had not arrived home, so the elders offered the mission CD to the wife. She accepted the gift, but told the missionaries that their CD player hadn't worked for five years. As she left the room to attend to the children, the elders sat down at the living room table and placed the CD player on it. Elder Forrest was especially adept with electronics (and later used this skill in his career). He inserted the disk and tried fiddling with all the various buttons and switches. Nothing worked. Feeling strongly that the music on the mission CD could truly bless the home with a better spirit, the elders decided to say a prayer. Both elders knelt down and quietly prayed that the CD player might work once again. After the prayer, Elder Forrest inserted the mission CD, just as he had done before. This time, however, it played. When the mother came out of the back room and heard music, she couldn't believe it. She said they had taken the CD player to three different places to have it fixed and no one had been able to repair it.

The husband returned home after the elders left and was surprised to hear the delightful sounds of the mission recording. As he sat down on the couch, he removed the CD insert and read along through all of the words of the songs.

The wife later reported to the elders that her husband listened to the CD all night long, "crying like a baby." The husband said that the CD reminded him of all the special feelings he had while serving his mission. The following day, he took the CD over to his mother so that she, too, could be inspired by the music and message. When he returned home, he tried to play some of his other disks on the player, but surprisingly, no other CDs would work. He requested another mission CD and found that it was the only disk that would work on his player! Elder Duncan concluded his letter by saying, "That is one powerful CD!"

I was awestruck that the elders would care so much about this inactive family that they would humbly exercise their faith to summon a miracle on the family's behalf. I was also heartened that the Lord would hear and answer their faithful petition, and that our CD music could reawaken this lapsed member to his buried tender feelings about the gospel.

Kika

Soon after I received word from Elder Duncan and Elder Forrest about the CD player, I shared their story at the Taguatinga Stake conference on May 16, 2004. The following day, two Brazilian elders left early in the morning to teach a new-member discussion to a struggling, less-active member who had attended the stake conference. The woman had asked the missionaries to come by at 6:30 in the morning that Monday, their Preparation Day, because it was the only window of time she could offer. Humbly, the missionaries complied. When Elder Silva and Elder Santos arrived for the discussion, there was a small dog sitting on a table. The elders had been there for only a few minutes when the woman's five-year-old daughter accidentally knocked the dog off the table. The dog landed headfirst on the hard floor, lapsing into convulsions before going completely limp. Its body stiffened and its tongue hung out to the side. No one could detect the dog's pulse, although at first they could hear some low noises coming from its throat. Everybody in the family was distraught.

A few moments passed. The woman finally said that she had heard me relate the story at stake conference the previous day about missionaries saying a prayer over a broken CD player. So she asked the elders if they could please bless her dog, Kika, reasoning that a dog was more important than a CD player. Her request shocked the elders. But after they looked at each other, they agreed to do it. The elders lifted the dog into their arms and blessed it together. Elder Silva, during his part of the blessing, blessed the dog to get up and be fine at the end of the new member discussion.

After giving this blessing, the missionaries felt they should go to another room in the house, where privately they offered an earnest prayer to begin a fast for the dog. When they returned to teach the woman, they started out by playing "Oh Lord, My Savior" on the CD, inviting everyone to sing along. The Spirit was very strong during the discussion, according to all reports. Still, the dog lay stiff on the floor the entire time, with its tongue—now black—hanging out to the side. Someone offered a closing prayer to end the discussion, and then, as prophesied, the dog jumped up! It wagged its tail, ran to get something to eat, and then started playing as usual. The family shed tears of delight.

Later, during our final meeting with departing missionaries, Elder Silva repeated this story to us and said it was one of the most outstanding experiences of his mission.

Several things about this story inspired and impressed me. For one, these elders gave up their Preparation Day in order to help the struggling woman. They had sufficient faith not only to invoke the healing blessings of the Lord upon the dog, but also to announce that the dog would be fine at the conclusion of the lesson. They even opened up a day-long fast *after* the healing blessing had already been given, and *after* the announcement of the timing of the dog's revival had already been made. These two elders were not steeped in priesthood protocols; they only wanted to help as asked and were willing to sacrifice in order to help. I was inspired by their faithfulness and courage. It was gratifying to hear that the first story about our mission CD played a role in helping this family to muster the faith necessary for their own miracle. Perhaps miracles are contagious.

The final vignette involves an investigator named Djalma, who was a Baptist pastor. Elder Camargo related this incident in his weekly letter to the president.

A Glimpse into the Future

"Pastor Djalma is a very good man who can help the Church here a lot. We have already reviewed almost all of the missionary discussions with him, and he could understand them very well . . . [he] said that everything that we said was true and that the Book of Mormon was also true.

"I was surprised one day while we were in his house conversing with him a bit. At the end of our conversation we placed our mission CD on his CD player for him and commenced the music. Then, and I don't know why or how, I had a vision of him in the temple, dressed in temple robes and doing his endowment ordinances. I couldn't believe what I was seeing. I shut my eyes and rubbed them, and then opened them again to the same vision. A second time I shut my eyes and rubbed them, and the vision was closed. It lasted only a few seconds. Wow! I became very happy and it gave me the desire to shed tears of gratitude . . .

"As you know, President, he has been the pastor of the Baptist Church, and he is in search of the truth. Each time that we visit him, we feel a very strong and sweet spirit. He told us that he would attend the general conference broadcast with us. We hope that he may be touched by the Spirit and get baptized quickly; that way I will be very happy indeed."

Two weeks after receiving this letter, I received a telephone call from Elder Camargo reporting that Pastor Djalma had decided to be baptized. He said that the key to his conversion was his attendance at general conference and being able to hear the words of the prophets there. He now wants his entire family to join and to be sealed. His baptism will probably occur when they can be baptized together.

I felt very grateful that the music would invite the Spirit for this elder so that he could have a brief vision of his investigator's potential. We saw firsthand how the Lord could use music to touch people's hearts and to prepare them for spiritual experiences.

Elder Nielsen, the exceptional singer mentioned earlier, was promised in his setting apart blessing that his musical performance would touch many thousands of lives. My missionary companion—my wife!—when set apart for her mission by Elder Craig Zwick of the Seventy, was told that she would go beyond the customary roles of her calling and use her talents in different ways to reach and bless the lives of many. She, too, reached many thousands.

Among the many mission responsibilities that my wife handled, she also organized a choir of English handbells, which performed around Brasília during the weeks leading up to Christmas. As a member of the American Guild of English Handbell Ringers (AGEHR), Mary Jane had years of experience with handbells and had insisted that we drag all our handbell equipment to Brazil with us. Our missionary handbell choir comprised thirteen missionaries, sixty-one handbells, and thirty-seven choir chimes. Each missionary was responsible, on average, for playing some seven or eight instruments. In the short time they had to practice, usually on preparation days, the missionaries mastered those instruments in stunning fashion. At that time, most Brazilians had never seen a handbell choir before (we called them *sinos de mão*) and they were enchanted by the novelty. Invitations and opportunities for the missionaries began to pour in.

Elder Ricardo leading handbell choir at the Federal Court of Justice, Brasília

The missionary handbell choir played at stake centers and shopping malls for the community and at gala events such as the dedication of the National Post Office Headquarters. One highlight was the opportunity to perform captivating and fun handbell arrangements of *Away in a Manger* and *Jingle Bells* on local and national television. The television host also interviewed me as part of the presentation. But it was a special honor to be asked to perform for the esteemed Federal Court of Justice in Brasília at its annual Christmas celebration. At the conclusion of the performance, a noticeably moved presiding justice arose to address all of the judges, officers, and staff. He said, "I hope you not only appreciated the transcendent quality of the music of these young missionaries, but that you also noticed the light that flowed from their glowing countenances. They exemplify exactly what we aspire for our young people of this country to be."

Missionary handbell choir playing live on television on the "Monica Show."

Chapter 12

FAITH-THEMED CONFERENCE AND ITS AFTERMATH

Of all our needs, I think the greatest is an increase in faith.

(Gordon B. Hinckley, "Lord, Increase Our Faith," *Ensign*, Nov. 1987, 52–54.)

Around the time we started distributing the mission CD, I learned an unexpected lesson at a zone conference—one that truly startled me. It was near the end of the March 2004 meeting when I announced, "Now I'm going to finish by sharing some thoughts about healing blessings." A chapel full of missionaries pulled out their notebook and pens.

Everything had gone wonderfully so far in our faith-themed zone conference. The missionaries had completed their reading assignments[11] for the meeting, and I had supplemented the material with a discussion about Elder Richard G. Scott's three sure pillars of faith. The Spirit was electrifying, both for the missionaries and for me. Realizing that we still had some time before taking a taxi to the airport, I decided to take advantage of the remaining moments and share another idea that I thought they might appreciate. I chose to offer some remarks about healing blessings, which could serve as a capstone for the entire

11 I had assigned the missionaries to read a chapter entitled "Building a Powerful Faith," from *To Him That Believeth*, by Frederick and June Babbel (Cedar Fort, Inc., 1997, available at http://bit.ly/1W6l1b2), and the book *On Wings of Faith* in its entirety (by Frederick and June Babbel, Cedar Fort, Inc., 1998) in English or Portuguese, and also a BYU devotional talk by Professor Richard H. Cracroft, "Divine Designs: Tracing the Lord's 'Pattern in All Things'" (Brigham Young University devotional, Dec. 10, 1996), speeches.byu.edu.

conference. This would be my chance to share a paradigm I had developed over decades of experience and reflection on the topic.

I was about to explain the degree of faith we could exercise when we called upon the Lord for healing. If circumstances fulfilled any of five conditions (which I would identify for the missionaries), one could act with assurance that with sufficient faith the Lord would grant healing, based on my analysis. There may have been some aspects of the mission that had me flying by the seat of my pants, but not when it came to this particular gospel hobby!

From the podium I could see that everyone was poised to take notes. Forty sets of eyes steered their gaze toward me. It was time to speak, but something strange seemed to be happening—I couldn't find the words.

I stood at the microphone, speechless while the missionaries stared. The drone of the ceiling fans was the only noise in the non-air-conditioned chapel. The Spirit was very strong in that moment—it seemed to be pressing up against me, nudging me from my foot all the way to my shoulder, and leaning against my right ear to communicate an urgent message. In that instant, I gained an entirely new understanding of faith and healing. The Spirit that had come upon me so suddenly left me sure of one point: however convincing my theories might be on the topic, however logical and carefully considered, I was *not* to present them. My understanding would actually serve to limit or even undermine the faith of these young men and women, and furthermore, my conclusions were simply incorrect! Then the Spirit emphatically and clearly communicated to me something I will never forget: *There is no limit to what can be accomplished by faith!*

I stood silently at the podium and pondered what to do for what felt like a few minutes, although it must have been only about thirty agonizing seconds. One of the things that the Spirit communicated to me was that even though I shouldn't present my theory, I could decide for myself whether to heed that prompting. As the silence continued, I quickly pondered what course I should follow. On the one hand, I had just announced to the missionaries that I *would* present it, and I wanted to keep my word to them as they were all expectantly waiting. On the other hand, the Spirit was strongly encouraging me in another direction. I finally announced to the missionaries that for some reason, I felt that I was not supposed to speak on the announced topic. I simply told the missionaries: *There is no limit to what can be accomplished by faith*, closed my talk in the name of Jesus Christ, and sat down.

Most of the missionaries had no idea what had just happened. Others seemed to perceive that the Spirit had constrained me in some way. One of the sister missionaries who witnessed exactly what was happening asked me afterward what had been whispered to me in my right ear by that spirit being who was "more glorious than the rest" while I stood at the podium. One elder told me that he had seen many spirit beings at the conference and described where they had stood or sat and what they were doing. (I saw nothing but definitely sensed and received a clear message.)

While almost everyone in attendance pondered the abrupt ending to my remarks, I was more surprised than anyone. To think that my theory and analysis of faith, so thoughtfully conceived and carefully developed, could actually be harmful for the missionaries was jolting to me. Awkward though it was, I was thankful to be stopped from saying something inaccurate or incomplete—something that could lead the missionaries to an incorrect understanding of such a vital principle.

The idea that faith needn't have limits became an inspiration, both to the missionaries and to me. It made a great difference in our work. After the conclusion of this round of zone conferences on faith, "all heaven broke loose" in our mission, and a showering of miracles continued for about six months at a level I had not seen before.

What follows are some examples of healings in our mission, many which occurred after the conference. A few occurred before but were reported to me after the conference, confirming what we had learned about faith. The healings in these stories differ somewhat in process and timing, just as in the scriptures we can read of healing processes that vary from touching the Master's cloak, washing in the river, or having clay rubbed over their eyes. A striking element of all of these stories, however different the details of the healings, was the unwavering confidence in the Lord, even in the face of great tests. The idea that there is no limit to what can be accomplished by faith resonates with each example.

Knee Cured

"Hi, President. How I loved this last conference on developing a powerful faith!" wrote Elder Raimundo in a weekly letter after the event. "It was very good, and I could feel the Spirit very strongly. When you were speaking, I was encouraged to relate something that happened to me on this mission, which I had not related heretofore so that you would not become worried.

"At the beginning of my mission, I began to feel pain in one of my knees, and the pain was increasing with the passage of time. [Knee, foot, and back problems often plagued the missionaries because they usually walked between five and ten miles per day.] When I was returning from that conference where you distributed some materials from your father on faith [which occurred about a year before the faith conference mentioned in this chapter], I was not able to walk right anymore. I began to read those experiences about faith and thought, this too can happen with me.

"One day while having lunch, my knee was in extreme pain. I looked toward my companion, Elder Di Rocha, and said, almost crying, that I was afraid I'd have to leave my mission and return to my home because of my knee, and he replied: 'Did you read the things the president gave to us?' I replied, 'Yes.' He responded, 'Then do the same thing. When we get home, offer a prayer and then work as if nothing was wrong with your knee.'

"That is exactly what I did. I prayed, and then we left the house to work. That day my knee really hurt, but we were working as if nothing was wrong with it, and the next day when I awoke, there was absolutely no pain at all, my knee was completely cured! Today I can work even better than when I arrived in the mission field."

This next account comes from Elder Axelgard, who served with us during our final year in the mission. Mary Jane and I did not hear this story until after he returned from his mission and visited us. We were touched by the account and asked him to make his record available to us for inclusion in our mission history.

Healed in the Nick of Time

"While working in Gurupi, my second area, I started to notice a growth that was causing me discomfort. It did not prevent me from working, but I remember feeling pain from it on a regular basis. The growth worsened as the second half of my first transfer there drew to a close, and I asked my companion, Elder Bell, what the protocol was for surgery on the mission. His response was that missionaries were sent home for those procedures. [Moreover, if they had surgery performed in the USA, they were almost never returned to the Brasília Mission but were reassigned to a mission in North America—if they were able to continue at all.] This added worry to my discomfort—an effect probably worse for a missionary needing to focus and forget personal problems to best help others. As the transfer ended, the issue had become foremost among my long-term concerns; should I stay and risk a more serious, perhaps internal threat to my health? Or should I volunteer this information to Sister Babbel [who was in charge of the missionaries' health] and probably get sent home? At the time, I was loving where I was (both geographically and spiritually) and would give anything to stay and work with those people.

"I knew that I could make a decision with Heavenly Father's help. I also knew from our mission training that I had to be very specific in what I asked in order to receive the appropriate answers. I spent a few days formulating the correct question in my personal study, and once I had it, I knew it was the right one and took it to God. Kneeling down one morning before personal study, I asked Heavenly Father, 'Am I going to be okay if I wait until zone conference to mention this problem?' The answer was a clear and comforting 'Yes.'

"With that off of my chest, I went back to work with gusto. The pain was still there, but with my prayer answered, it was almost like a slightly uncomfortable, constant reminder that I could forget about myself. The following six weeks were fantastic, and the looming zone conference did not prevent us from achieving miracles that shaped the rest of my mission. Ever since I suffered with dengue fever in my first area, Sister Babbel had the habit of asking me specific questions regarding my health whenever she saw me. I had made the decision not to lie to her. But even if the growth was there, and she asked, and I told her the truth, I knew I would be okay. We took the bus up to Palmas, spent the evening on exchanges with the local missionaries, and before going to bed (on the night before zone conference) I checked and found the growth still there. In my nightly prayer, I closed with a reminder to Heavenly Father of the promise I received and of the confidence I had in it. I awoke the next morning, and there was no trace of the growth. Sure enough, Sister Babbel asked me about my health, and I replied with a smile that I was being helped in that regard. Almost a year and a half later I remain healed."

At our final meeting with the departing missionaries in June 2005, we learned that another elder's mission would have been cut short if it weren't for the Lord's intervention. Elder Camargo shared a story at that meeting about something that had happened to him during the first two months of his mission. The following account is taken from my notes as Elder Camargo spoke.

Boils Be Gone!

"During this early part of my mission, I developed severe boils on the soles of my feet. I would limp around with my companion so that we could do missionary work, but the boils were becoming increasingly painful and I had more and more difficulty walking. I finally reached the point one night where I could walk no more and had to be carried home by my companion.

"That night, I explained to the Lord in a prayer that I had been called by prophecy to serve a mission, and that I simply could not do it in my present condition, as I had become immobilized. I prayed for the Lord to remove and heal my boils so that I could go about the work to which I was called. I then got in bed and went to sleep.

"The next morning when I awoke, there was no trace of boils anywhere on my feet! I had been completely healed—the boils had been removed from me, just as I had requested in my prayer. For the rest of my mission, I never had any more trouble with my feet."

Like Elder Camargo, Sister Lucas and Sister Zimnerman trusted in the Lord's ability to heal. Their faith was so great that the Lord could not restrain his blessings from them, even though the initial blessings that they received did not grant a full healing. I'll begin with the story of Sister Lucas, taken from a weekly letter.

A Healing Blessing

"On Tuesday we went to Paraíso, even though I wasn't well, to attend a district meeting. At the end of the meeting, I asked that the elders give me a blessing of health. Elder Ries said in the blessing that I should not be concerned, because the disease I had was passing. However, I desired an immediate resolution to my infirmity.

"It was then that I asked my companion, Sister Bezerra, if I could offer a prayer together with her. Then, we knelt and I prayed with all of my heart, asking Heavenly Father that He cure me, because I knew that He could take away my infirmity if I exercised my faith. I cried much during my prayer, but was immediately comforted with such a strong feeling of peace, such that I felt as if a hand touched me and removed from me all of my infirmity. From that moment, I no longer felt any pain, but rather, a renewed force to continue the work of the Lord. What a blessing!"

The fact that she wasn't afraid to ask for more help after her blessing impresses me. It shows a deep understanding of the power of personal prayer and a steady determination, which the Lord clearly recognized and rewarded.

Back Issues

We saw a similar miracle with Sister Zimnerman, a professional model in Brazil and Portugal prior to her mission. Apparently all of the walking during her mission exposed a serious physical condition. She sent me a weekly letter that disclosed a severe back and pelvic bone problem, and even though I didn't understand the anatomical issues very well, I knew that she faced mission-ending surgery. About two weeks later, she wrote me another letter, saying that she was healed. When I interviewed her, she explained the entire story to me—when it all started and how she had recovered.

While serving her mission, a problem was uncovered in the way her back, posterior ribs, and pelvic bones were interacting. It was suggested that she undergo corrective surgery, but she felt it was not necessary. But after serving a year, the problem got much worse. She was able to walk only with a lot of pain, and she was unable to carry anything. Then, as her condition continued to degenerate, she could work for only a part of the day. It reached the point where she could not work at all because it was too painful for her to stand and walk. She finally took a bus to Cuiabá, four hours away from Cáceres, to seek some competent medical help. The doctors performed a series of X-rays and confirmed that she had a congenital condition in the formation of her posterior ribs, spinal column, and pelvic bone and that all of her walking had caused the condition to deteriorate to its present state. She was told that she should undergo surgery immediately, and that her recovery period would be about two months or more.

Sister Zimnerman was unwilling to have surgery performed, as she realized that it would result in the premature end to her mission. She prayed and then asked for the zone leader in Cuiabá to give her a healing blessing. To her disappointment, she received a blessing that told her she would be given enough strength to withstand the pain. She was then able to walk a little, but with considerable pain.

Sister Babbel and Sister Zimnerman

Sister Zimnerman went to the zone conference the next day in Cuiabá and we spoke of developing a powerful faith. (The conference was similar to the one mentioned at the outset of this chapter, and part of the series of faith-themed conferences.) We handed out a translation of a chapter from my father's book *To Him That Believeth* (CFI, 1997) entitled "Building a Powerful Faith." On her bus ride back to Cáceres, she read that chapter, which contained examples of healing through the exercise of faith. Sister Zimnerman said to herself, "But I have faith, too!" She then decided to exercise her faith to receive a complete healing by offering up mighty prayer. The next morning she said that she no longer felt any pain, and was in good condition to work. For the remainder of her mission Sister Zimnerman worked without any pain or difficulty. She was even able to train a new missionary during her last six weeks in the mission.

I admired Sister Zimnerman's tenacity to exercise faith to obtain a full healing, when the initial blessing was only that she would be able to work with pain. Fourteen years later, as this book was going to press, I contacted her in Brazil and inquired about the condition of her back. She reported happily that she had been completely healed and that the problem had never recurred!

The stories of Sister Zimnerman and Sister Lucas show that sometimes the Lord heals through degrees. For some reason, He withheld a complete healing from them through the priesthood blessings they received but healed them completely once the sisters prayed on their own and exercised faith. These stories remind me of one occasion recorded in Mark 8:22–25 of how the Savior needed to offer two blessings before the blind man's vision was fully restored.

While healings sometimes happen by degrees, other times, they are immediate and unmistakable. The following example is one (of many) that shows that priesthood blessings do indeed have the power to grant full healings.

Take up Thy Bed and Walk

Elder Harbuck wrote in his weekly report this moving account of a miracle that he witnessed:

"Last Saturday morning, I felt inspired to pass by Ana Paula's house. So we went there and found her family very receptive to the gospel. Ana Paula is the only member so far in her family. Her mother, Maria, had faith enough to mention at the close of the lesson how she wished that her husband, Adão, would be able to walk again. She even explained the accident he suffered a few years ago which has left Adão in a wheelchair and also without a regular ability to speak.

"Feeling so inspired, I prescribed the following: to have one member of the family fast each day starting that day after lunch and in six days we would return and give the blessing so that Adão could walk again. The Thursday night prior to the blessing, we did a special family home evening on faith with Adão and Maria, and those of the Elders Quorum in the branch who will participate in the blessing.

"I wrote the following that same day: 'In a few hours, we will give the blessing. This promise has so diligently filled my mind throughout these past few days that I have already seen [in my mind's eye] Adão take up his wheelchair and walk.' Nonetheless, I did not know whether the Lord would sanction the healing until just two or three minutes prior to giving the blessing, when the Holy Spirit confirmed this to my mind.

"Sure enough, I sealed the anointing and pronounced the blessing, feeling inspired to promise him that he would walk with his two legs (with no aid necessary) . . . and that his speech would improve in understandability. After the blessing, Adão sat in his wheelchair for a moment and I broke the silence, 'Now it's up to you to walk.' So he wheeled over to the wall to get his bearings, stood up, and walked to me, ten feet away from where he was. His legs are still very weak and his balance was still iffy, but he walked. And he even walked into church the next Sunday to the gratitude of some members of the church."

In a subsequent communication from Elder Harbuck a month later, he stated, "Adão is speaking better and continues to walk well. Because Church is about three miles distant, he prefers to catch a ride when he can." Later, he updated me: "Now, almost four months later, Adão continues to be a walking miracle."

Truly, the Lord fulfills His promises to His servants:

> For I am God, and mine arm is not shortened; and I will show miracles, signs, and wonders, unto all those who believe on my name.
>
> And whoso shall ask it in my name in faith, they shall cast out devils; they shall heal the sick; they shall cause the blind to receive their sight, and the deaf to hear, and the dumb to speak, and the lame to walk. (D&C 35: 8–9)

Throughout the course of our mission, we saw the gifts of healing richly manifest among missionaries, members, and non-members. In the case of the missionaries, were it not for their faith, we would have been compelled to send home many more of those who were suffering from debilitating health problems, including each of the elders and sisters whose health concerns were discussed in this chapter. I have not attempted to cover the full range of healing that happened over the course of our mission because it was so broad in scope, nor have I included most of the recorded healing miracles. While the scope of what can be achieved through faith extends through many realms besides healings, this was one way that the truth was manifest that *there is no limit to what can be accomplished by faith!*

Chapter 13

MODERN MIRACLES

And it shall come in a day when it shall be said that miracles are done away . . .

Mormon 8:26

"Today the libraries would bulge their walls if all the miracles of our own time were recorded," said President Spencer W. Kimball in 1981.[12] It's a shame we don't hear more about these miracles of our time. We would have a clearer picture of the Lord's interest in us if we recorded and shared the times we received heavenly help. It can be difficult to recognize miracles in a world where we don't wait anymore for manna from heaven; we go to the supermarket or to Walmart.

The stories in this chapter involve (among other things) a sprinkler hose, a digital clock, an electric grid, and the music blasting from a Brazilian "sound vehicle." That's one of the fascinating things about modern miracles—they can look different than the wonders we read about in the scriptures. The accounts in this chapter have convinced me that the Lord is willing to act in behalf of His children, often in ways I never would have thought to request.

President Thomas S. Monson said, "When faith replaces doubt, when selfless service eliminates selfish striving, the power of God brings to pass His purposes."[13] These stories show that it takes faith not only to ask for heavenly help, but also to recognize it when it comes instead of explaining it away.

---

12 "President Kimball Speaks Out on Administration to the Sick," *New Era*, Oct. 1981, 48.

13 Thomas S. Monson, "Willing and Worthy to Serve," *Ensign*, May 2012.

A Sprinkler Hose

Difficult family circumstances forced Elder Quêvedo to drop out of school as an adolescent. He faced many physical hardships growing up in central Brazil, and less than two years prior to his mission call, he suffered a severe skull injury from a car accident in which he nearly lost his life. However, he was blessed with spiritual gifts that more than compensated for these limitations. The following is one of two of his experiences that I have included in this volume.

"Yesterday we had a baptism. We arrived at the chapel around five p.m. to fill the baptismal font. But there was no water. From the font's faucet, the only thing that came out was [a trickle of] very brown, dirty water. At that juncture, a thought came to my mind: 'Trust in the Lord. Everything will work out fine.'

"However, I began to get frustrated and asked Heavenly Father, 'Why is this happening? Is it not Thy will that a baptism take place here today?' At that point, another thought came to my mind—that I should get the hose that was being used to water the grassy area of the church's garden. I mentioned this to our ward mission leader, but he said that my suggestion wouldn't do any good, because the hose was full of little holes so that it could be used to sprinkle the lawn. Therefore, he went down the street to see if he could get another hose from one of the nearby neighbors and members.

"I was already completely wet because it was raining outside, but I had to arrange for water to fill the font in some way because the baptism had been announced in Sacrament Meeting and it wouldn't be long before the members would begin to arrive. It was at that time that another thought came to my mind, together with an order: 'Get that hose in the garden and cut the end off of it and then fill the baptismal font.' Therefore, I did it. [Note: sprinkler hoses are sealed at their end to force water through the tiny pinholes to create the sprinkling effect.]

"I am grateful to Heavenly Father. The baptism was very spiritual and the font filled up very well, and even though I used that sprinkling hose from the garden that was full of small holes for watering, hardly any drops of water leaked out of those holes while I used it to fill the font."

I note here that because Elder Quêvedo had very little formal education, he was unaware that water would flow through the opening that gives the least resistance. But the Lord knew this, and Elder Quêvedo knew enough to trust in the Lord. I was particularly touched by how explicit the inspired directions that he received were. I believe that the Lord cares very deeply about these baptismal services, thanks in part to Elder Quêvedo's report and what I witnessed in a later experience in Miracema, Tocantins.

Getting in Tune

In order to attend a baptism in the town of Miracema, I had to travel about six hundred miles from the mission home—a trek that included an airplane ride, a long drive in a rental car, a ferry ride, and a journey through an Indian reservation. I didn't mind the long trip because I was thrilled to witness the long-awaited baptism of the Santos family. Several pairs of elders had worked with this family over the years, and although they helped the teenage son to join the Church and prepare for a mission, they never managed to capture the interest of the father, who was a pastor in the Assembly of God faith, as well as a part-time politician and auto mechanic. I felt strongly that this family could be key to the growth of the Church in Miracema. I sent Sister Pierce and Sister Stevens there, specifically to work with the pastor and his family. While the son was away serving his mission, these missionaries worked with his parents and his sisters. After a prolonged period of investigating the Church, the family, including the father, decided to be baptized (with the exception of one of the sisters, who was baptized later), and I was able to witness firsthand the experience at the baptism that Sister Stevens recorded.

"For the baptismal program, I chose to sing 'I Know that My Redeemer Lives' without knowing that this hymn is one of their favorites . . . Our new investigator, Romaryo the musician, who was to accompany me on his guitar, wanted to practice with me prior to the start of the program and tune his guitar, but he was delayed. When he arrived at church, the baptism was about to begin, so we just ran through it really quickly but to our dismay, the guitar was completely out of tune. Indeed, it was so far out of tune that I felt it nearly impossible to sing the melody correctly. But President Carlos, being a new [branch] president and perhaps a bit nervous because of your presence, said with urgency that the time for practice was already expired and that the baptismal service needed to begin immediately."

I had watched the rehearsal between Sister Stevens and Romaryo before the baptism began. The practice session was disconcerting, to say the least! The guitar was far out of tune—enough so that virtually anyone could have perceived the same. I tried not to grimace or furrow my eyebrows as I listened, and was preparing to restrain myself again as the meeting began.

Sister Stevens continued, "I told Romaryo not to worry and that everything would work out. I sat there praying the whole time. At the appointed time, we went ahead and performed the music. After the baptism, Romaryo looked at me with tears in his eyes and said, 'The Lord tuned my guitar!' It was incredible. I know that the Lord's hand was in that."

The guitar really did play in perfect tune, and the overall effect was sublime. I had no idea what was going on behind the scenes, but after learning about it, I marveled that the Lord would somehow see to it that the baptismal services went on without a hitch, even the musical number. We truly have a very kind Lord who can rescue not only troubled souls, but troubled music, too. This experience moved Romaryo deeply. He shortly thereafter also joined the Church and, after waiting the requisite time period, served a mission in Brazil. As for Pastor Santos, he eventually became the new bishop of the ward (which had been a branch at the time of his baptism).

The Vulgar Sound Truck Incident

Elder Anjos had a wide grin on his face when I saw him at mission headquarters one morning. He was anxious to report an unusual experience that he had earlier in the week.

He and his companion were on their way to an important lesson to their prime investigator family. They had been praying fervently that the Spirit of the Lord would accompany their teaching, so that the lesson would reach the investigator family with power. They were doing all they could to maintain a good spirit en route to the lesson.

As they neared the home of their investigators, a sound vehicle passed in front of them. A sound vehicle is a common form of advertising in Brazil, especially in smaller towns. It's a truck or car mounted with several loud speakers that blare the sound of an announcer to the neighborhood, usually traveling very slowly so that the neighborhood can hear the entire announcement before the vehicle moves on to the next neighborhood. Between announcements, the sound vehicle typically plays loud music to attract attention. This particular sound vehicle was blasting music with loud and filthy lyrics in English—words which even a Brazilian such as Elder Anjos understood because of his knowledge of English.

He reported, "They were disrupting the spirit we were trying to maintain. My companion, Elder Tuttle, became enraged and shouted in a loud voice toward the vehicle, 'Shut up!' At that very moment, the vehicle broke and the sound turned off completely. The driver emerged and tried to get the vehicle to operate again and turn on the sound, but he could not get it working at all. Cool! We were very surprised.

"As we returned to that location after delivering the lesson, we encountered the driver still by the side of the road in the same spot we had left him. He was tinkering with his vehicle and trying to get it re-started!"

Now I cannot say for sure that it was the hand of the Lord that assisted in response to the "directive" that Elder Tuttle issued, but I've heard of enough experiences like this one in our mission that it wouldn't surprise me at all if it was. In this case, I don't see anything wrong with what occurred. In fact, this story left me grinning, too.

The Timed Discussion

Elder Quadros was serving in the same community where my wife and I were residing when he related this story to me:

"We had an interesting experience last week while presenting a first discussion to a family.

"The man, Marcelo, is in the military. We conversed a little with him and as we spoke about the message we wished to present, he asked how long it would take, and I responded, 'Approximately 30 minutes.' He then pointed to a digital clock on his stereo console, which showed hours, minutes, and seconds, and said, in a very serious tone, 'I am counting; your time has already begun.' He did not call his family to join in the discussion.

"We thereupon began to lead the missionary discussion, and quickly lost track of the time, but he didn't lose track, because he frequently looked over at the digital clock to check the remaining time. As we were recounting Joseph Smith's First Vision, our time was about to expire. There was less than a minute left of the allotted time when we heard a slight noise and the digital clock stopped, its lights dimmed and turned off by themselves. Marcelo didn't notice this but later, after we had finished the story, he looked over to check the time and was really shocked that the stereo's indicator lights continued to function but that the clock had stopped and gone dark. He did not know at exactly what time the clock had stopped working. He said, somewhat mockingly, 'Look at that, the clock even stopped. It must be something from the Lord!' He started messing around with the plug and then pressed various buttons on the stereo, to no avail, and finally used the remote control to get the clock to light up again.

"But when he managed to turn on the clock again, he saw the point at which it had stopped—it had stopped only about five seconds prior to the 30-minute deadline he had imposed on us. He turned white! It was really cool, as he said in a voice that was slightly trembling, 'Did you see that? You can continue, I won't be counting time anymore.' He then summoned his family to hear the remainder of the lesson."

Shower Power

The following story from Elder Chase made me smile. It's an example of the kindness God can show when we make an unusual but sincere request.

"We have been having water problems the past little while to the point that we have not been able to take showers some days.

"I finally got so fed up with it that I knelt down and said a prayer and asked for the water to come back so I could take a shower.

"Since that day I have not only had water, but usually hot water. The water never works for my companion, Elder Santos, but always for me, whether I take a shower first or he does! (Actually, I did tell Elder Santos about what I had done but he didn't believe me. He called it luck.)

"Miracles happen, even in the mundane things of life!"

Brigham Young said that we live far beneath our privileges,[14] but who would have thought that our "privileges" extended to a nice hot shower? Apparently Elder Chase did, and he reaped the rewards by exercising his faith.

Let There Be Light

I was interviewing Elder Moraes on the final day of his mission when he made an off-handed comment that caught me off guard. He asked what I thought of the "incident" of Elder Gonçalves up in Sinop, as if I were familiar with it. Elder Moraes was surprised that I had not heard about it and proceeded to give me his own account of what had transpired several months earlier when he and Elder Gonçalves were companions for a brief period. After I heard the story, I asked the president of the Sinop Branch about it, because he had been an eyewitness to what had happened. President Jorge confirmed the story in all its particulars. Finally, I spoke to Elder Gonçalves about the incident. He had not included any information about it in his weekly letters to me, which wasn't surprising because he was a very humble elder. Upon my direct questioning, however, he verified the story, and later provided interesting details from an entry in his journal, a portion of which I include in my account.

Elder Gonçalves and his companion joined the branch president and his wife on the terrace of the chapel one evening, there to teach a middle-aged mother and her teenage daughter. The mother was an inactive member of the Church who had stopped attending shortly after her baptism several years earlier. She knew very little about the Church and her daughter had never become acquainted with it.

As related by Elder Gonçalves and confirmed by the others, "We were on the terrace conversing about the power of the priesthood. The inactive woman

---

14 "There is no doubt, if a person lives according to the revelations given to God's people, he may have the Spirit of the Lord to signify to him His will, and to guide and to direct him in the discharge of his duties, in his temporal as well as his spiritual exercises. I am satisfied, however, that in this respect, we live far beneath our privileges." (*Discourses of Brigham Young*, compiled by John A. Widtsoe [Salt Lake City: Deseret Book, 1925] 50.)

responded that she did not believe that missionaries had that power to perform miracles. I testified to her that we indeed did have this power, coming from God. As soon as I had uttered those words, the lights in the chapel went out. From the terrace, we noticed that the energy had been cut from the entire city, or at least that portion of it which was visible from the chapel, including all of the downtown area and surrounding suburbs." This was not uncommon in Sinop where sometimes the energy would stay off for hours, or even days, while at other times it would return quickly. "The sky was so black, [as happens at that hour in the tropics] that we could see nothing. All we could do was hear one another's voices. We could not enter the chapel and present our missionary lesson under such circumstances." After waiting a few minutes for energy to be restored, the city remained in total darkness. The elders, investigators, branch president, and his wife continued their conversation while awaiting the possible restoration of electricity to the city.

Sinop Chapel and courtyard

Elder Gonçalves's journal entry then states, "As we continued conversing on the terrace, I told the inactive woman that the priesthood could indeed perform any kind of miracle through God's power. She repeated that she did not believe in such things. Then I received a prompting of the Spirit in my mind: 'Tell her that you will use this priesthood to cause the lights of the city to return.' At this first prompting, I was startled and cringed at the thought. A second prompting then came, this time to my ears, saying 'Vaiiiiii! Você consegue.' [Loosely translated, this meant 'Go ahead! You will succeed.'] I felt the Spirit very strongly in me, and told her that 'The power of the priesthood is so real that by that power I can make the lights of this city return.' She replied, 'I doubt it!' I felt strongly confident that the lights would return. Therefore, I stated: 'I will count to five, and upon reaching the number five, I will snap my fingers and the lights will be restored.'"

Elder Lessa and Elder Gonçalves

To everybody's shock, he then began counting. His companion, Elder Moraes thought, "Only two things could happen from this, and one of the potential outcomes is not good." Again, from the diary of Elder Gonçalves, "I began to count 'one, two, three, four . . .' and as I did, the voice of the Spirit whispered again in my ears, 'Você consegue!' Upon reaching 'five' I snapped my fingers. At that instant, the lights came back on throughout the city. Everyone was amazed, especially that inactive woman." Elder Gonçalves wasn't surprised, because he had heard a voice affirming that he could perform that miracle. The group then entered the chapel and the elders presented the lesson. The daughter was later converted and baptized, and the mother began attending Church once again.

I have thought about this experience many times. It reminds me of Nephi, building a ship, who described the matchless power of God by saying, "If he should command me that I should say unto this water, be thou earth, it should be earth" (1 Nephi 17:50). Elder Gonçalves felt the Spirit of God telling him twice that he could bring the lights back on, and because his purpose was worthy, he went ahead and did so. Why he happened to count to five and snap his fingers, I don't know, but he said that was what he felt impressed to do.

What a blessing it was to work with faith-filled missionaries like Elder Gonçalves—missionaries who lived worthily enough to listen to the inspiration of the Holy Ghost and allowed it to direct their work. Imagine what could happen if we were always so aligned with God's will and followed it fearlessly!

A Strange Electrical Grid

On the other geographical extreme of our mission, about a thousand miles from Sinop, lies the town of Posse, an agriculture-based community of about thirty thousand people on the border of Bahia. Traveling between the two municipalities during our mission required three bus trips and consumed about fifty hours including layovers (but not including the usual breakdowns)! Although Sinop and Posse are far apart, they share common ground in our mission's history. Blackouts and shortages regularly plague the electrical grids of both cities, and because of this, both Sinop and Posse have seen the missionaries exercising faith in curious ways.

In Posse, a very faithful member named Deborah shared one of her dreams with the missionaries while they were having lunch at her home. From Elder Harbuck's account, I quote: "She had woken up three times in the last week, in the middle of the night, with the name of one of her recently widowed neighbors in mind. She asked us what this meant. 'You need to talk to her!' was our response, which she soon fulfilled." Deborah scheduled a discussion with her friend for an evening when the elders already had something planned, but they scrambled to work out exchanges so they could fulfill both commitments.

The surprise occurred on the way to the home of Deborah's friend. "Shortly before arriving at Deborah's friend's house, all of the power went out in the small city of Posse, as seems to occur quite frequently. Every house except Deborah's friend's house was dark. We entered the house and taught the lesson at the Lord's request. Some of the neighbors even came over to see what was going on, probably intrigued that her house was the only one on the electrical grid that actually lit up. (The house had no backup generator.) At the conclusion of our lesson, we departed the house and energy was restored to the rest of the surrounding neighborhoods."

The city lights (or lack thereof) stories from Sinop and Posse involve inverse manifestations of electrical phenomena. In one case, the entire city lit up at the missionary's behest, while in the other case, only a single dwelling had light. Someone who doubted the miraculous nature of the first experience might claim that it was a matter of luck, and that the timing of the elder who counted to five was serendipitous. I think the second one would be harder to explain, though. When considered against the backdrop of the stereo console clock that stopped mid-discussion, the sound truck that malfunctioned upon command, and the CD player that suddenly worked again (but only when playing our mission CD, as recounted in Chapter 11), it strikes me that there must reside in heaven an exceptional repository of electronic wizardry. And to think that it would be summoned in behalf of these faithful missionaries is remarkable!

Pause the Rain Now!

In the final year of our mission, we received several hundred copies of *Preach My Gospel*, a new system of missionary learning and teaching that we were directed to implement. The manuals were printed in color on very high-quality materials. The report below is from Elder Rawle, who was charged with taking the manuals on a five-hundred-mile bus trip northward to our missionaries laboring in Tocantins, our most tropical mission area. The books had to arrive in time for a scheduled multi-zone conference the next morning where they would be introduced and the missionaries would be trained on how to use the exciting new system.

"Elder Axelgard and I left our house to grab the shuttle bus into Brasília, where we would meet up with Elder Drury and Elder Forrest so that we could [all] head to the state of Tocantins for our conference. It began to rain slightly, which put us in a predicament. We had no umbrellas, we were already behind schedule so we could not return to our apartment to get them, and we had a bunch of open boxes containing all the new mission materials that could not get wet. So I said a quick prayer out loud as we hurried down the street. I asked God to stop the rain for about ten minutes so we could find a bus or van into Brasília.

"All of a sudden, the rain stopped. After rushing about for some time, we found a van and got in. Almost immediately afterward, the rain began to fall in torrents. Elder Axelgard was sure that it would be raining in Brasília, which would prevent us from meeting the other elders. So I said another prayer, silently this time. Sure enough, the rain stopped just as we got to Brasília and we were able to meet the elders without incident.

"Yet in spite of our best efforts, we were still late getting to the main bus station. The bus we needed for our eighteen-hour trip should have been leaving right as our taxi pulled up to the station, and we hadn't even picked up our reserved tickets yet! I said another quick prayer, asking the Lord to delay the bus. I shouldn't have been surprised when I arrived at the ticket counter and learned that our bus was behind schedule, and that we would still be able to catch it.

"As I reflected on this experience, I could not help but feel a little like Jacob when he wrote, 'We can truly command in the name of Jesus Christ and the very trees obey us, or the mountains, or the waves of the sea' [Jacob 4:6] . . . Truly, the Lord's hand is in this great work."

Chapter 14

THE SECOND MILE

Sacrifice brings forth the blessings of heaven.

William W. Phelps

Besides hearing about the Lord's tender mercies for the young missionaries, one of the things that made me happiest was reading in their letters to the president about the times they decided to make extra effort. To be sure, the missionaries were already doing an impressive amount of work. They regularly spent twelve hours a day, six days a week, on the job. Preparation Day was hardly a vacation; they often had to spend a good portion of the day cleaning their apartments, buying groceries, washing clothes (sometimes by hand), and writing letters home, before they were expected to be out the door working again by dinnertime. And yet, some of these missionaries decided to give even more. The first story in the chapter is my own—a surprising experience I had with the extra effort of one particular mission zone.

Ambushed by the Spirit

One sultry October morning in tropical Tocantins, my wife and I entered the Palmas Chapel for a zone conference and began walking up the aisle toward the stand behind the pulpit. We had barely seen anything but the backs of the missionaries when the Spirit of the Lord suddenly seemed to wash over us, overwhelming us both. By the time we arrived at the stand, our eyes were full of tears.

I was embarrassed to be so emotional before even reaching the stand to start the meeting. I didn't dare look at my wife because I knew I would lose my composure—what little there was left! I looked down and tried to hide my face from the missionaries but it was of no use. The tears kept flowing.

A letter from one missionary later helped me to make sense of the incident. Sister Chapman wrote, "We [our mission zone] fasted to have the Spirit of understanding to know what we could do to help our areas. We also fasted for you during conference time so that you could be inspired by the Holy Spirit. The week before that conference, we were challenged [by our zone leader] to pray for one hour each day. We would arise early or go to bed late to pray to the Most High. We prayed that we might receive His instruction from you at conference. That was a powerful thing for us to do. Those prayers were hard on our knees but they strengthened our faith. We did so to know more completely the will of God."

As we looked out upon the missionaries' faces that morning, our feelings of love for each of them overflowed. Sacrifice, dedication, and love were visible in their countenances. They were clearly aglow with the Spirit of God.

It was with great difficulty that I spoke at the outset of this conference. I had to simply block my awareness of this Spirit so that I could gain sufficient composure to speak in an almost-normal voice. We felt ambushed by the Holy Ghost because we were completely unaware of the missionaries' prior preparation!

Just as the Lord honored the fast of these elders and sisters serving in Palmas, He blessed our other missionaries as they gave more than what was required of them. Take, for instance, the story of Elder Bezerra, who was faced with a dilemma about how to spend Preparation Day.

Sacrifice Brings Forth Blessings

"President, I would like to share something that I learned yesterday," he wrote in his weekly letter. "During our weekly planning session, Elder Larsen and I saw that we had an appointment at eleven o'clock in the morning with a man who could meet us only on Monday. For that reason, we were thinking that we should reschedule our Preparation Day from Monday to Thursday for that week. But then we had the impression that we were treating the subject as we would with some ordinary kind of work where you schedule holidays. We then resolved to go ahead and work on Preparation Day and it resulted in the best day of my mission.

"The lesson with this man was so good and so spiritual that we left there on cloud nine. It was my best lesson thus far. Afterward, we went to have lunch and along the path a woman stopped us and asked what it was that we did, and so we made a marvelous contact. At night, a member took us to the home of a family to introduce us to them and we discovered that it was a 'golden family,' ready to hear the gospel message.

"With these facts I can consider that yesterday was the best day of my mission. I am very happy. We thought that we would become very tired for working on Preparation Day, but this did not happen. I remembered your lesson about giving our best to the Lord, a full 100%. I am grateful and happy to know that Heavenly Father blesses our efforts."

Elder Reid and Elder Freire also decided to spend their Preparation Day in a novel way—preparing! They spent the day in gospel study, companionship gospel discussions, and prayer. The result was that they had unknowingly prepared themselves for a marvelous service to perform.

A Shining Example

Elder Reid wrote, "At the conclusion of our Preparation Day [and after an evening of proselyting], we came back to our home around 9:30 p.m. and found a note on the floor urgently asking us to [telephone] José Alves. We went out and called him, only to find out that there was a certain boy who needed a blessing of health. His name was Herbert, a boy eleven years old. He was in the General Hospital of Gama. Although the boy was a non-member, his member aunt asked that we give the blessing. It was late and dangerous, and the hospital was on the other side of town, so we decided to wait for the next day.

"The following day, right after district meeting, Elder Freire and I went to the hospital. Using the written note we had been given as a pass to get through the gate (there were lots of people outside), we walked around asking the nurses if they knew Herbert. Nobody knew him. The place was absolutely packed with portable beds and IVs in the hallways, and the people were afflicted with all manner of disease.

"In the large main room, the view was even sadder. There were so many people. No privacy. Nobody knew Herbert. We kept going through the people to the other side of the room. Finally, we found a nurse who knew who he was. She gave us some breathing masks and started to walk. The nurse explained that he was in an isolated section of the hospital, and that the doctors were suspecting spinal meningitis. She went and opened the first door—there was a little sink to wash your hands in. She then cautiously proceeded to open the door behind to reveal a small little room, uneaten food on a desk, and a young boy sleeping on his bed. The boy's condition wasn't too good. He could never stay awake at all, and the times that he woke up he complained of his head and stomach. Meningitis, from what I understand, swells and inflames a part of the brain and pinches the spinal cord, shutting off the nervous system little by little. Herbert had undergone a procedure to drain away the cerebral liquid. He had already lost all feeling in his leg and could not move it anymore.

"The nurse told us two things: (1) 'We're not responsible for anything that happens beyond this door'; and (2) 'The more time you spend inside, the more dangerous it gets.' We went in and shut the door behind us. As I took the [consecrated] oil out, Elder Freire woke the boy gently and asked permission to give a blessing. With the boy's consent, Elder Freire did the anointing. During the anointing, there was a dark and grave feeling that came over me, as if I were being told, 'No. He's not going to make it. You shouldn't bless him with health . . .' But the moment I laid my hands upon his head to give the blessing, this warm, peaceful feeling of love and compassion flowed through me, giving me the feeling that the Lord's ever-watching eye was over him, and that as our Father, He loves and cares for him very much. I felt that the Lord would see him through these difficulties and continue to bless him afterward. I conveyed these feelings into words, telling him that he would get better. He didn't hear any of the words. That did not matter to me. In fact, the boy was asleep the entire time except when the non-member grandmother walked in with a breathing mask between the anointing and sealing portions of the blessing. She was present during the sealing of the anointing. Afterward, all three of us left together.

"After the blessing we explained to his grandmother outside that blessings depend upon our faith in Jesus Christ. This had been a tremendous lesson to me of the truth and power of the Holy Priesthood, that the Lord never has too many patients, that He is the doctor who can cure us all if we but come unto Him.

Elder Reid continued, "A week after the blessing, the member aunt sought out both of us to talk personally with us. She related that from the moment we gave Herbert the blessing, he started waking up more, eating more and talking with his family. We learned that the boy was deemed sufficiently well that he was able to leave the hospital shortly thereafter."

Elder Reid believed that the extra efforts helped prepare him and his companion to do this service. "Elder Freire and I would study every Preparation day for 5–6 hours and just do companionship study. Consequently, when we left our apartment that morning to deliver the blessing, we were both filled with the Spirit, and ready to go out and work. We were feeling very strong." I have seen so many wonderful results happening when the missionaries are willing to go "the extra mile" that I am convinced these efforts demonstrate to the Lord the extent of our faith, and underscore our love for Him and our fellowman. Such efforts are often pivotal to how He responds.

The following excerpts were taken from the letter of Elder Teixeira, who saw for himself what happened when he followed the inspiration to keep going at the end of one very long day.

"The Stupidest Decision I Ever Made"?

The story began earlier in the week, when a young woman working at a bakery noticed Elder Teixeira and his companion and asked, "Excuse my curiosity, but what is it that you do?" The elders explained that they shared a message about the Lord's plan for His children, and it was designed to strengthen families.

She breathed deeply and said, "I think this is what I am needing in my house." The elders then invited her to hear the message, but she demurred, saying that she had a young child who was a lot of work and that she didn't have the time.

Elder Teixeira was sad at first that she seemed to reject the message outright, especially when she thought she needed it. After pondering it some more, he arrived at the conclusion that "the Lord has his own time for everything, and that when the right time arrived for that family, He would provide a way."

The day ended and a new one began. The elders spent the entire day teaching lessons and paying visits to people. "As our working day came to an end," Elder Teixeira wrote, "we were exhausted. We got home at about nine p.m.; I had a bad headache, blisters, and chapped legs from walking all day in the heat. But we still had one thing left . . . We had scheduled a visit in the house of Sister Sônia, President of the Relief Society, to resolve some problems that were happening with our lunch calendar. She lived a considerable distance from our house, and given that it was late, and that we were as tired as we were, this was a visit we really did not want to make at that time. [Editor's note: These missionaries didn't have telephones.] We thought of visiting her on the next day, but something said to my heart that we must leave that very moment.

"Sincerely, this appeared to be the stupidest decision I had ever made in my entire life. There was no necessity to leave at that hour of the night. It was already late and we were so tired, and the route to her house was dark, deserted, and at times dangerous; these factors did not help me understand why I had that feeling that we must go there, but at last, we resolved to leave.

"Along the way we encountered a man seated on the sidewalk, at the edge of the road with a bicycle thrown in front of him. He had his head bowed and the first impression I had was that he was drunk. Once more I felt something that led me to make another decision against my will. I felt that I must speak with him, even though he was drunk. When we approached him we had a big surprise. He wasn't drunk, but rather, crying! His eyes were very reddened and he appeared to be completely without hope. We introduced ourselves to him and asked him what was happening and how we could help him.

"He told us: 'I am trying to kill myself, I already have thrown myself in front of a few cars, but all of them swerved around me.' We asked him why he was doing this. He replied that he was having many problems at home with his wife and he could not stand to live that way any longer.

"I felt the Spirit very strongly at that moment, and everything began to make sense. I could perceive why the Lord sent us out of our apartment in spite of all of those negative circumstances.

"We explained to him about our message and the importance of families in the God's eternal plan, and because of the importance of the family to God's plan, we were severely tempted and often had difficulty in dealing with certain problems.

"We conversed a lot with him and at the end, he said, 'Wow! It must have been God who put you in my path because a few minutes ago I wanted to kill myself and now I am even smiling.'

"We took him to his house and scheduled to visit him the next night. But the most interesting part of this story was yet to come . . .

"When we reached his door the next night to visit him, we could not believe what we were seeing. We were met by his wife, who was that same young woman we had encountered the previous morning at the market, and who declined to schedule a visit with us even though she knew that she needed the gospel in her life. Once more I could sense the sweet feelings of the Holy Ghost testifying in my heart of the veracity of the restored gospel of Jesus Christ."

It's amazing to me that one tiny decision—the choice to settle the lunch calendar with the Relief Society president—perhaps ended up saving this father's life and bringing the gospel to him and his family. I was grateful that these elders had the resolve to keep on going when they were tired, heeding the Spirit that inspired him to go through with this last appointment. It is never "stupid" to follow a true prompting of the Holy Spirit. The key is to recognize the prompting and discern its divinity. This can be difficult at first, but gets easier with experience and as our discernment develops.

Chapter 15

FAMILY MEMBERS ON THE OTHER SIDE

The spirit world is not far away. Sometimes the veil between this life and the life beyond becomes very thin. Our loved ones who have passed on are not far from us.

(Ezra Taft Benson, *Ensign*, June 1971, 33)

The idea that family members from the spirit world anxiously attend our missionary work often struck me as true, but it wasn't something I understood very deeply until I experienced it myself. (The "Protection" chapter shares one such instance.) I learned that sometimes the missionaries sensed such help, and sometimes the people they were teaching experienced the distinct support and presence of a departed one. The first story is one in which I *felt* unseen support from the other side, but that some people with a spiritual gift could *see.*

Relating the Rebecca Bean Story

In May of 2003, I was speaking to about three dozen missionaries at a zone conference in Tocantins. My topic concerned the sacred nature of their callings. To illustrate the point, I read a testimony that my great aunt, Rebecca Bean, had recorded four decades earlier. This great aunt died in 1976 and I never met her, but I have often pondered her story and sacred experience. She and her husband had been called to live in Palmyra, New York, in 1915 to help acquire and manage properties for the Church. Throughout their nearly twenty-five-year-long mission in the birthplace of Mormonism, their residence at the Joseph Smith home served as a gathering place for any members or missionaries visiting the area.

While my great Aunt Rebecca Bean was living there, she had a very sacred experience that taught her the value of missionaries in the Lord's eyes.[15] As I stood at the podium recounting her powerful testimony, I felt something very strong. I had the distinct feeling that she was there near me, standing a few feet away to my right, bearing witness to the truth of her sacred vision and testimony. The feeling completely surprised me. When I spoke a few seconds later about how we must not denigrate our callings by improper behavior, I felt an incredible spirit all around the pulpit, and only with difficulty could I deliver the rest of my message.

Rebecca Bean

After the conference, I received a letter, dated May 18, 2003, from Sister "Katia," a wonderful Brazilian missionary. She wrote the following:

"President Babbel, I would like to speak about the conference. I liked it a lot, and learned much about making outlines, about revelation, and I liked the challenge [you] gave [us]. When you were speaking with all of your feeling about us being representatives of Jesus Christ [just after having related the Rebecca Bean testimony], I know that I saw angels surrounding you, and their light was seen. Your countenance shone and the light of angels radiated. There were many of them with you."

After the conference, another missionary gave me a verbal account of what he saw, confirming the presence of the spirit of a woman near my right side and bearing testimony as I spoke, as well as the presence of other spirits. I marveled that Rebecca Bean's testimony and sacred vision were confirmed to some missionaries in this matter.

15 Her vision and the marvelous circumstances surrounding it are recorded by her grandson in *A Lion and a Lamb*, Rand H. Packer, Spring Creek Book Company, 2007. See an abbreviated version of her testimony here: https://ldsscriptureteachings.org/2016/12/08/rebecca-beans-experience/.

A Lost Child

Just as I knew that we were not alone in that moment, Elder Manfré sensed that somebody was helping him when he led a discussion with a family one night. The mother and father of the family had lost one of their children in a tragic accident.

"We began to teach them and the Spirit with us was very strong. At times I was incredulous at the words that were coming from our mouths as we spoke by the Spirit. Then my companion [Elder Homer] began to speak about eternal families. The intensity of the Spirit became stronger and stronger, and I began to feel something different—a feeling of great peace. Next, I saw and felt the presence of a small child. In that room I perceived a very strong light and I could discern the appearance of this small child. My words became stronger with respect to how this man could reunite with his child after this life. With tears in his eyes, this man told us that the hope that one day he could see his child again gave him the desire and strength of will to cope with the death of that child. I don't know how to describe with words the feelings that I had but I know that for a moment, the veil was opened and I saw and felt that light—a child that was not with us in physical matter, but in spirit. Shortly thereafter the father of this child handed to me an album with some photos of his child. I almost cried, because I was very certain then that it was the same child that I had just finished seeing and feeling.

"Experiences like these motivate me and strengthen my testimony that the world of spirits is often not far from us."

Angels Will Attend

Another missionary, Elder McAllister, saw the conversion process draw a family together from both sides of the veil as well. He witnessed this as he taught Maria do Carmo, a woman who had worked for the bishop's family as a housekeeper. I asked him to recount the experience after his mission for my own records:

"When we arrived, it appeared that she had been anticipating and preparing for our visit for quite some time. Her house was immaculate, she was wearing very nice clothes and she had bought dinner for us to eat as we talked. She was a single mother of two young adult children. Her husband had died when they were a very young family, leaving her to fend for herself and the children. She loved her husband deeply and had never remarried, even though by this time she had lived about nine years without him. She had very little formal education, and had worked long hours as a maid, doing dirty, hard work to put her children through college—something she wished she had attained herself. Her heart was as pure as gold. We left after our first discussion with great hopes that she would be baptized in the near future.

"However, despite her welcoming attitude, she distanced herself slightly from embracing the message during our second discussion. She was a slow reader, and it seemed that she had a hard time grasping some of the principles we taught her. I personally think we were so excited after our first discussion that we left her with too much gospel homework. She had a heart of gold, but I think she was not very educated in literature. Our teachings seemed complicated and didn't sink in all the way.

"We desired more and more to help her understand, and spent great efforts to explain principles clearly, simply and concisely (a difficult thing for me). We prayed with great fervor and sincerity in her behalf. During the discussions I remember trying with all I had to follow the Spirit in order to best understand and teach her.

"One night, she told us how much she loves her husband and how sometimes she is filled with desire to know how he is. She prayed to know how he was doing and to know if she could be with him again. She told us about a peculiar dream she had after praying on one occasion to know if he was all right. In her dream, she 'crossed over to the other side' and was permitted to see her husband. I believe she said he was dressed all in white and looked wonderful and happy. He indicated that he was permitted to speak to her and had two things to say. He told her that he was well and happy, but that he was so sorry he couldn't be with her again after this life. I felt the Spirit so strongly and felt as Daniel must have felt interpreting the king's dreams. The Spirit immediately explained the dream to me, and I jumped on the opportunity to explain. I explained that he said that they couldn't be together again if she continued in her present course. She needed to be sealed to him in order to be together forever. If not, what he said would come true. We taught about eternal marriage and how a family could be together forever. I don't think we had explained authority yet, when something amazing happened.

"I didn't see anything, but I knew distinctly that there was an angel in the room behind me and to the side. I couldn't hold back tears from flowing. I realized it was her deceased husband and felt an urgency from that corner of the room. I felt this urgency so clearly and tangibly that it overwhelmed me. I almost heard his voice in my mind urging me to teach on.

"I told her what I felt and testified that I knew it was real and true. We explained again about the Spirit and how she could know too. (Elder Santana also seemed to feel something strong from the Spirit.) We taught her as much as we could under the direction of the Spirit, and closed with a prayer and an invitation.

"As we walked away marveling together, I prayed in gratitude, and the same overwhelming certainty washed over me again. I heard in my mind her husband pleading with us to go back and teach her. I think I heard the words 'go back' six times. 'Go back. Promise me you will go back and teach her.' I understood at the time he meant for us to continue teaching her—to not give up, even if she struggled to understand. I promised him.

"My mission ended before she came to church once, but I did get the chance to make a return visit with Elder Brown and President Babbel. I felt the Spirit again very strongly and left her in the hands of Elder Snell and Elder Rodrigues to teach. I don't know the outcome, but I learned several things that night."

One of the things I learned from this account is the way we partner with heavenly beings as we share the gospel. The hopes of these departed family members for the living ones can breathe purpose and urgency into the work we do. They will not forget their loved ones.

Family members from the spirit world can make their presence felt quite powerfully during a sacred ordinance, as we see in the next two examples.

Baptismal Experience and Genealogy

Elder Marques and Elder Fort, who were working in Santa Maria Second Ward, had an interesting experience during the baptism of Maria Aparacida, a mother of four children who had all been baptized earlier. I compiled this experience from their written accounts and interviews.

Maria Aparacida waited almost two years before she felt fully prepared to enter into the baptismal waters. On her baptism day, one of her daughters, a girl of fifteen years of age who had already been baptized into the Church, saw her deceased grandfather there. He was in the water with his eyes fixed on his grandchildren in attendance, standing almost in between Elder Marques and Maria Aparacida, his daughter. When the girl saw her grandfather's spirit, she clutched her chest and blurted excitedly, "Veja! Há avô!" ["Look, there's grandfather!"] It was as if he, too, was trying to be baptized. The granddaughter immediately started to cry.

Following the baptism, the girl told her mother and the elders what she had seen. After hearing the story from the granddaughter, Elder Marques obtained all of the vital information about this man, and with the family's enthusiastic support, made plans to perform the vicarious baptism for this man in the Recife Temple after his mission.

Baptismal Service Attended by Ancestors

Sílvia de Jesus had already been baptized, but due to a technicality in the registration date of her marriage, she needed to be re-baptized six months later. At this second baptism, only seven or eight people came to watch. Elder Jacobson shared part of his journal entry about the baptism with me.

"I'd have to say that this was probably the most spiritual baptism that I've experienced in my lifetime. Elder Cássio bore his testimony and it seemed to be from the heart. After that, we sang two special hymns, 'Faith in Every Footstep' and 'In the Baptismal Waters.' As we sang, it seemed as though a legion of God's angels were singing with us. It was powerful. It was interesting—the whole time we were there it sounded like there were quite a few other people in the church. I looked around and couldn't see anybody. Three times I looked around the chapel to see where the music was coming from, but could see nothing. I then walked down the hall to see if there were others in the [building] that were singing, but there was nobody in the hall, nor in the rooms alongside the hall.

"After she was baptized, while changing into dry clothes, I felt the Spirit very strongly telling me that we weren't the only ones there, that many of her deceased ancestors were there—people who are waiting, I believe, for the vicarious work to be done for them. I saw how important she will be and is to so many." Sílvia de Jesus threw herself into genealogical work after the baptism.

Later, Elder Jacobson supplemented this account with more details in an email. About the choir that sang at the baptism, he wrote, "I don't know how to describe it other than that the voices were perfect, they were clear and crisp and were accompanied with strong feelings of love. From what I can remember, they sang with us in Portuguese, but what I know is I could understand them perfectly. Singing with them was an enormous blessing and sacred privilege."

This example struck me for the way that the ancestors seemed to outnumber the actual mortals at the baptism. Since this particular baptism was a do-over, perhaps fewer people attended, but there was no damper on the celebration in heaven! It reminded me that in all of these priesthood ordinances, "the power of godliness is manifest" (D&C 84:20).

Glimpse and Transformation

These reports from the missionaries confirmed to me that our work is more of a team effort than we know, and more important to our family on the other side than we often recognize. I close with a powerful experience that I had at a zone conference, which helped me to feel much closer to my recently deceased father.

I was talking to the missionaries in Cuiabá about the end of my father's life – a period of time when he was battling Alzheimer's and I was offering a lot of prayers for him. My father's anguish reached the point where he received help from beyond the veil to comfort him. My journal entry for that day reads, "As I related [to the missionaries] my experience, I felt something that I had never before felt with such sublime power and intensity—a tremendous and sustained outpouring of love and understanding from my father for my well-intended petitions in his behalf—a love that eclipsed anything I had experienced. My father conveyed to me clearly that he was fully aware of my prayers in his behalf during that period of illness. I sensed that the kind of consuming love my father was transmitting today was a portion of the Lord's divine love, and it thoroughly penetrated my soul. The feeling was so exquisite that I will seek the rest of my life to be worthy of partaking of it again. I wouldn't trade it for anything in the world!"

Unbeknownst to me as I spoke, some of the missionaries in the audience were having a variety of their own confirming witnesses. They were able to sense, by different degrees, that something special was happening. I found out about the first spiritual experience from my wife, who spoke with two of the missionaries, Elder Souza and Elder Lessa, after the conference while I was doing interviews. They approached her excitedly and asked her a number of questions, like whether my father had a different complexion/skin tone than me, what his hair color was, how the pitch of his voice was different from mine, and other questions about his characteristics. My wife assumed she must not be understanding their Portuguese correctly because the questions were so unusual! But she understood that they felt they had seen my father.

Later, Elder Souza and Elder Lessa met with me, and I recorded their experience in my journal that evening. They said that "as I spoke in zone conference that day, they both separately saw me enveloped in an exceedingly white light, with my shoulders, hair and face shining very brightly. They said that the tone of my skin was transformed, and that my voice took on a different quality and somewhat higher pitch—as if I were no longer the person who was speaking, but someone they surmised to be my father. They both felt certain that somehow the spirit was that of my father being manifest, but they wanted to verify it through a description of his physical characteristics, such as his hair and skin tones. They said that the light waned and then grew brighter a second time during the latter part of my talk. . . . They also said that they saw light upon the heads of several of the missionaries seated in front of them during the conference. They reported that the background wall behind me was a variation of a transcendently beautiful green and white. Neither of them had ever seen anything like that before." (There were no sunrays coming through the windows. The heavy, completely opaque chapel curtains were drawn fully shut due to the oppressive heat in that area and no air conditioning.)

In his weekly letter, Elder Souza summarized the experience more briefly, but added two interesting details, as follows:

"We went to a zone conference today in Cuiabá. President Babbel spoke about the experiences his father had, and the Spirit of the Lord confirmed to me all that was being said. Then, out of the blue, the thought came to my mind, 'I want to see his father.' This same thought came three times. Then, suddenly, the appearance of President Babbel changed, as well as his voice. I looked around the [sacrament] table, and on top of the heads of some of the missionaries was a white crown. The shirt of President Babbel began gleaming brightly, and his hair turned white. I felt the Lord's Spirit very strongly.

"I asked my companion if he had sensed something different at that conference. He replied that he did. I then asked him if it was in relation to the father of President Babbel. He replied that it was. He then began to relate his own experience, which was identical to mine."

Shortly after this event, I received a letter from one of the sisters in attendance at the conference, Sister Brewer, who was at the end of her mission. An excerpt of her letter, written on an airplane as she returned to the United States, follows.

"I want you to know that in our last [Cuiabá] conference as you talked about your father, I had a really sacred experience where I saw him in you. I came to know him for a brief moment and I will forever be grateful to him for raising his son as he did. I know because of that experience that one day, when the veil has been lifted, I will recognize him and be able to thank him personally."

Years later, in a separate email, Sister Brewer reminisced about her experience and added some interesting detail: "I was sitting by myself on the last pew and I still remember how it felt when I looked up and saw your dad in your place. I kept blinking my eyes expecting it to go away. I honestly don't remember anything you said that day but I've never forgotten how it felt to be a part of something so powerful and sacred."

Another missionary, Elder Richardson, mentioned that the Spirit was like a thick film and was almost palpable, although he did not experience any vision.

We are blessed with different spiritual gifts, and we come into these moments with our own unique preparation, desires, and context. It's no wonder that sometimes our spiritual experiences come with different degrees of clarity. I was grateful for spiritually sensitive missionaries who enriched my understanding of this experience with their witnesses, especially because I didn't see anything myself.

We read in the New Testament and in the Doctrine and Covenants of the many gifts of the Spirit that are given to mankind. Among them we are told: "[To] some is given, by the Spirit of God . . . [the gift of] the discerning of spirits . . . And all these gifts come from God, for the benefit of the children of God." (D&C 46:17,23,26. See also 1 Cor 12:10.) While relatively few have the gift of discerning spirits, yet the rest of us can gain insights from those who do. One of the most gratifying things about worshipping in congregations and serving missions with others is the opportunity for sharing and benefitting from the various spiritual gifts that are sprinkled among us.

Chapter 16

SAVIOR, SOURCE OF LOVE

If with all your hearts ye truly seek me, Ye shall ever surely find me, Thus saith our God.

(Aria No. 4 from Félix Mendelssohn's "Elijah")

God is love.

1 John 4:16

I know of no force in mortality as strong, no power so infinite and personal as the Savior's love. Some of the missionaries wrote about times that they felt this love to some degree. When they did, their feelings of fear, ill will, despair, frustration, and doubt dissipated almost immediately. I treasure the letters they wrote and the lessons I learned from them—that the Lord's love can scatter dark feelings, leaving the recipient transformed and grateful.

The following stories about the Savior's love differ in context, but in each one, the recipient was quickly transformed so that nothing else seemed to matter.

"The Morning Breaks"

I placed the Brazilian elder who wrote this letter in an area of our mission that was failing rapidly, in a ward with such a spirit of apathy that it was hardly functioning anymore. Although I did not disclose this sorry situation to the elder at the time I transferred him there, he perceived it quickly. He told this story in a weekly letter to me:

"We have ten new members who are each day going more inactive because they are not receiving what they need at Church: a friend, a responsibility, and the nurturing good word. We had a ward missionary who served well, but her companion did not help. Therefore, the good one asked to be released . . .

"Last week I felt weak as sadness and discouragement consumed me because there are so many abominations and such iniquity here in this suburb, even that which involves members. I began to pray, asking for strength to overcome all of these feelings of despair. Many thoughts crossed my mind, even a wish to end my mission and return home. But the desire I have to serve the Lord helped me avoid doing anything so drastic. I prayed to the Lord and implored for His help. Yet I arrived at a point where I found myself feeling unworthy to renew my covenants with the Lord.

"There was so much iniquity and gossip, and all of these things were getting to me. It was a trial so great that I would not be able to endure the pain in my bosom and I could no longer view anyone as a brother, because everything that they were doing was wrong. Even my companion seemed to be doing everything wrong—in our companionship study, our planning, our visits—everything seemed to be under an evil force bent on destroying my mission, and even my own life. But I continued to pray, asking for strength, asking for pardon if I had done something wrong. I got to the point of asking the Lord to remove me from here.

"On Sunday, I woke up very confused, and we went to Church. When the time for the Sacrament arrived, I thought that I would not partake of it. I thought that it would even worsen the situation. But I knew that I was not unworthy, it was just that I did not know how to explain the pain that was suffocating me.

"When I received the bread and placed it in my mouth, I was unable to swallow it. Therefore, I remained with the bread in my mouth, thinking of Jesus Christ and all of his suffering and the pain he underwent in their behalf and in my behalf. I then swallowed the bread and for me it was like a medicine with amazing curative powers—everything that was bad went away and what remained inside me was a very peaceful feeling, a peace so sublime that it completely transformed me. I love these people and know that Christ is the one who changed my heart, allowing me to love the sinner but not the sin.

"Today I am happy. I know that Christ lives."

"The Shadows Flee"

Sister Prado, the Brazilian sister missionary who penned the next report always struck me as a deep-thinking and valiant servant of God. She was the same missionary who prayed to be able to understand the English version of General

Conference (in Chapter 3). In a weekly letter to me, she explained how little things had caused her to lose the Spirit—arguments and cross words. Once she lost the Spirit, her feelings grew increasingly negative and she had to strive hard to feel the Holy Ghost once again. A portion of her letter follows:

"One of the ways of making a missionary of God lose her sensitivity to the Spirit is for her to think that she no longer possesses it and is not worthy of its presence. Then discouragement, despair and sadness begin to become a part of her thoughts, and a lack of self-esteem and a feeling of spiritual worthlessness become constantly apparent. When this happens, nothing seems to be working correctly, and only negative thoughts take over her mind. The missionary begins to question her calling, whether she is really in the correct place, and she begins to forget that her calling as a representative of the Savior has great value.

"This happened to me one day. I was not in tune with the Spirit of the Lord. I was focusing on the relentless heat and the idea that the physical sacrifice was useless. Numerous doubts and questions surfaced in my mind, such as

> "Why do I have to walk so much when I'm not seeing any results from my work?
>
> "Should I really be here on a mission?
>
> "Did I make the correct decision?
>
> "I don't think I am helping at all. What am I doing to help these people?
>
> "I wasn't prepared to come on a mission, so why did I come?
>
> "Is this really the work of God?
>
> "Many other unsettling questions passed through my mind.

"And thus it was, all day long. My companion knew that I was in a funk because our messages were no longer in harmony, and she knew that I was not feeling the Spirit very strongly. As we walked along the road, I had sadness in my face as tears fell from my eyes.

"We had a lot of work that day, and it was only 7 p.m. We still had four more visits to make. Everything was becoming so difficult and it seemed like my prayers did not ascend to the ears of Heavenly Father. I no longer felt that peace and happiness that I could normally feel. A lot of unsavory questions about my own worthiness and value came to mind.

"Once more, we left the house of a very special family but my feelings did not change. My companion looked directly into my eyes and asked, 'Sister Prado, would you like to go back to our home?' Her statement resonated strongly in my heart, and I perceived that the influence of my feelings of despair was affecting our work.

"I have never felt worse than having to return home early and as I watched my companion cancel our appointments by telephone, it made me even sadder. We returned to our house and for an instant I reflected upon all that I was feeling, and knew that day I was somewhat irked by my companion for having different opinions than me, but I never thought that this could turn into a problem. (D&C 10:20)

"I began to read the scriptures, but wound up sleeping.

"When I awoke, in the middle of the night, my heart still felt very tight and an enormous anguish took over me. I no longer wanted to feel this, so I knelt down and began to pray to the Lord with all of the strength of my heart. I explained to Him all of my feelings and asked Him if I really had been called by Him to participate in His work in this dispensation. I asked Him if He loved me and if He was by my side. I did not want Him to abandon me. I told Him that I was feeling so unworthy that day and I was unable to feel Him by my side, and that I no longer felt His Spirit. Once more I asked Him if He loved me and if I was really in the right place.

"Tears streamed from my eyes continually and I felt that this was one of those prayers where I was most intent upon obtaining an answer, no matter what the answer was. But to stay on a mission I needed to feel that I was doing the right thing. And with all of His mercy the Lord once more embraced my heart that night, gave light to my understanding, and it was as if the most loving being that existed, our Savior, took my hand and spoke to my mind: 'My daughter, you were called and are worthy for this work, never doubt this.'

"Peace returned to my heart, and I could feel an indescribable joy as a recipient of the Savior's love, because I know that He spoke with me that night and that He soothed my soul and helped me comprehend how important it is for us to remain strong in our trials and that we must do our best to have the constant presence of the Holy Ghost and not fall into the traps of despair.

"And more important than anything, I learned that He never abandons us. It is we who distance ourselves from Him, we who lose our sensitivity, and we who must try to learn always how to be used as instruments to do good works."

I was impressed by Sister Prado's faith to pray even when she felt unworthy. It was similar to the first example, where the missionary decided to partake of the sacrament, even when he wasn't sure that it would help. The darkness dissipated for both of these missionaries with these small acts of faith, and the Lord replaced their discouragement with peace and an assurance of His love. It is one thing to know about the Savior, but it is a greater thing to experience His love.

"Love One Another"

Although the Lord can certainly communicate in response to a direct prayer, sometimes His love comes through other people. The next story is a powerful example of how this works.

Elder Viera (pseudonym) had a difficult upbringing. He was raised by his grandmother because his own mother was an alcoholic and unable to care for him. When he was old enough to get a job, he paid for all of his mother's house bills, even though he didn't reside with her. He did not depart for his mission until he was twenty-six because of these kinds of challenges.

When I met Elder Viera, I sensed that he was insecure and tentative about serving a mission. I knew I had to pick a great trainer for him, and I felt inspired to call Elder Healey, who had already trained two missionaries and had proven himself to be a kind, able teacher as well as a very hard worker.

In a letter written after his mission, Elder Healey said that he felt awkward when he first met his new companion because of the vast difference in their backgrounds. Elder Viera was clearly from a less-fortunate situation. After a few weeks together, though, the two became good friends. "Elder Viera was a very tenderhearted individual who loved people and was as humble as they come," wrote Elder Healey. "He had some problems, and although I don't know exactly what they all were, I do know that he felt a little depressed at times with life. In essence, though, he was a man who just wanted to be cared for and loved."

One evening Elder Healey and Elder Viera went to teach an investigator named Vanessa (pseudonym) and her four children. Because Elder Healey had served in the area longer, Vanessa knew him much better than his new companion. To Elder Viera, though, it appeared that Vanessa and her family just didn't like him as much.

Elder Healey wrote, "While teaching a discussion to Vanessa and her family that evening, for some reason Elder Viera was having some problems. He was emotionally distraught and he got up and walked outside and sat on the porch that was just outside of their family room. I could see him and I wanted to go and talk with him, but decided to give him a moment to think. I continued teaching because I was in the middle of a lesson, and the Spirit was so intense that I felt like my heart was about to explode."

When the discussion ended, he and his companion started heading toward their next appointment. Elder Healey wrote, "I asked my companion what was wrong and his reply was 'nothing.' I asked him again, 'Elder Viera, what is wrong?'

"He responded, 'It is just that I am a Brazilian and I can't even teach as well as you can and it is my language.' I reassured him that he could, but he had to believe in himself. He then expressed that he felt that the people didn't love him as much and went on to tell me that he felt terrible, as if an evil spirit had entered his body. Of course, I set him straight on how the people felt about him. He was such a witty and affable young man who was easily liked. I sensed his frustration with these situations and wished I could help him.

"While we were walking in complete silence down the sidewalk that went [through] the middle of the town, I felt impressed by the Spirit to put a hand on his shoulder. I explained to him that the last discussion was so spiritual that I felt like the Spirit was carrying me. I told him that I was going to put my hand on his shoulder and that I felt impressed to do so by the Spirit. I explained that I felt that the Spirit was so strongly a part of me that it would transfer over to him and calm him. While walking down the sidewalk I placed my hand on his shoulder, and we both remained silent as we walked for about a minute. I looked over to Elder Viera and I saw tears streaming down his face. I asked him how he was doing, and his reply was 'I am okay.' He explained to me that he felt as if the Spirit had entered into every inch of his body starting from his head down, and that it took away all of the bad feelings that he had inside. His reply was remarkable to me and quite stunning because I never expected such a response. He said that it was like Satan had a hold of him and was putting bad feelings inside of him and that when I placed my hand on him the Spirit rushed in and put him at ease.

"We arrived at [our next appointment] and before going in, I told him that he would teach the whole lesson and that I would just add in some comments at the end. I reassured him that he was a good teacher and that he would do awesome. We entered [the] house and he taught a perfect lesson. The Spirit was present, and little did Elder Viera know at that time, but he would baptize [this investigator] just before he was transferred."

Elder Healey ended his account of the experience this way: "He taught me to have more patience and to love unconditionally. Maybe, just maybe I was able to see how our Father in Heaven feels."

I was tremendously thankful for Elder Healey's kindness, and for the way he showed Elder Viera what he was capable of doing. His example of Christlike love and respect is something we want to reflect to all we meet.

"By This Shall All Men Know"

Love not only builds confidence, it can melt hostility. Elder Freire thought he would be teaching only one investigator, named Rogério, together with his senior companion and the stake president. He didn't know that Rogério had invited seven of his friends to the discussion, most of them pastors from other churches who didn't take kindly to a pair of Mormon missionaries. His account follows:

"We sat down and my companion said to them that we were not there to debate. They replied that it was not their intention to debate either. When we got to the part of the discussion that treated the apostasy, my companion passed the teaching over to me. For the first time I refused because the Spirit was not there. The 'investigators' had bombarded my companion and President Samuel.

"Next my companion bore testimony, and one of them stood up and was possessed by an evil spirit. He went toward my companion and began to look into his eyes, saying that everything was a pack of lies. Next, he came toward me. I was afraid, but a voice came to me that said: 'Look into his eyes without any fear and bear your testimony.' And that is exactly what I did and that man ran away from that place.

"I expressed my love for them, got up and hugged each person, and they began to ask for pardon, confessing that they had been in the wrong. Three of them received the missionary lessons later with their families.

"The Spirit testifies, but love is what helps people recognize the Spirit. I have a strong testimony of this principle."

"Our Savior's Love"

This final example is from an elder who was serving in the most dangerous part of our mission. The missionaries in this area regularly ended their proselyting day by 5:30 p.m., when it was starting to get dark. They would then seclude themselves in their second-story apartment, sitting on the floor below the window level so that the random gunshots that occasionally began at that hour would not harm them! Even the police were reluctant to enter that area. We sent elders there because the valiant members in that area deserved missionary assistance, but the difficult circumstances often led the elders to do some soul searching. The letter from the missionary reads:

"I'm sorry that I was kind of weird in the interview, not talking and all, like I usually do. There is a reason for that, but to understand why, there is something I would like to tell you that is very special to me.

"This all started back in [city name withheld] where I was struggling with a lot of things—sickness, anger, frustration, annoyance of pushing another companion to work, and a whole lot of other things. A whole lot. Anyway, I found myself in constant prayer, asking for what I should do. And as I was praying at my bedside I felt the grip or the hold of another person hugging, as if we were standing up, but I was on my knees. I felt the hug stronger and stronger, and also a peace and comfort I had never before felt.

"I dared not open my eyes, and as the time passed by I just cried on the shoulder of this person, who I believe was the Savior. After I was comforted like this, I really had no more questions or doubts in my head about anything. I just want to bear my testimony that this truly is the work of God and that Christ truly comforts the ones that have weakness. I am so thankful for everything and the knowledge that I have gained here in the mission. I truly am thankful for leaders that help me stay active and for all these things in my life. I leave and end this with my testimony in the name of Jesus Christ, Amen."

His letter left me speechless and overflowing with gratitude. His story and the others in this chapter reminded me of the Psalmist's words: "Cast thy burden upon the Lord, and he shall sustain thee" (Psalms 55:22).

Our Savior's love is stronger than any negative feeling. It is simply remarkable! What a blessing it was that each of these missionaries developed a deeper understanding of the Lord's love for them and how this love could transform their efforts.

Epilogue

It may be less natural for inhabitants of a modern world to look heavenward when there are good hospitals, GPS, smartphones, and Siri. The temptation in this increasingly secular society is to believe that the Lord saved all His firepower for earlier times, even wondering if He indeed exists at all. The great prophet Mormon, perhaps responding to similar feelings among his fellow disciples, asked, "My beloved brethren, have miracles ceased? Behold I say unto you, Nay; neither have angels ceased to minister unto the children of men" (Moroni 7:29).

I know this is true, and the experiences in this book stand as a modern-day testament to this scripture. The Lord is just as invested in building His kingdom on Earth today as He ever was, and we were privileged to see that from up close.

Although a given missionary might experience only a handful of spiritual occasions during the mission, or perhaps none at all, yet from the perspective I was granted, having received and reviewed the weekly letters and accounts of over 500 missionaries during our three years of service, it was overwhelming. Moreover, in this volume I have shared only a tiny fraction of what I reviewed, and there were undoubtedly thousands of more spiritual experiences that the missionaries chose to keep private. When one considers that the Brasília Mission is but one of some 400+ missions worldwide, the cumulative effect of the Lord's assistance in missionary work can only be imagined as His servants search for people willing to hear His messages and experience His love. And when one recognizes that the Lord works through people of many faiths in His outreach to uplift all mankind, the scale of His work is truly unfathomable.

I close this book with three accounts. The first is about something unusual that happened at a stake conference, where the Lord's hosts reached out to the humble people in attendance with an unusual reflection of His love. The second demonstrates how the Lord honors those who serve Him. The final one motivated me to write this book.

Surround Sound

At our final stake conference in Brasília, I decided to speak about the alternative verses I had written to the well-known children's song, *I Am a Child of God.* We made copies of the lyrics and distributed them to the congregation ahead of time.

The new version, which was translated into Portuguese with the help of our friend, Thaís Maciel, gave a different theme to each verse. The first verse emphasized the importance of learning to perceive the voice of God—in essence, *knowing* His will. The second verse focused on *doing* His will, and the third stressed the importance of *being* holy people.[16] The version we wrote transformed a children's song about supplication to their earthly parents into the prayer of an adult seeking divine help from our Heavenly Father:

> I am a child of Thine, and precious in Thy sight;
> Each day I ponder on Thy words, they fill me with Thy light!
> Thou hast shown Thy tender mercies; gratefully I pray:
> Teach me all that I must know, to live with Thee some day.
>
> I am a child of Thine, my life I consecrate
> To do Thy will with humble heart, because Thy love is great!
> Lead me, guide me, walk beside me, help me to obey.
> Show me all that I must do, to live with Thee some day.
>
> Heaven is whence I came, my spirit is divine,
> By faith I can become like Thee—transcendent truths sublime!
> Send Thy love to purify me, seal my heart, I pray!
> As Thou art I'll strive to be—Come dwell with me this day.

After explaining the textual changes in my talk, I led the congregation in song while my wife played a magnificent accompaniment that she had arranged. As I was leading this song in the first session, strong emotions took me by surprise. The Holy Ghost entered me so forcefully that I was unable to sing the words for the first verse and half of the second, and ended up just whispering the words as if I were singing them. When we reached the final verse, the sound of the congregation seemed to transform into a lush, all-enveloping choir. The transformation to "surround sound" was pronounced and perceptible. The additional

16 These three themes were stressed especially by President McKay, President Kimball, and President Hinckley, respectively.

voices I heard were clearer, more beautiful, and singing on accurate pitch. They were voices of native Brazilians singing in strong unison, as Brazilians typically sing, yet there was something transcendent and angelic about the sound quality.

Although I mouthed the words while I was leading the third verse, I was so choked with emotion that I could not utter a sound. It occurred to me that perhaps I was privileged to hear, for a few moments, a heavenly choir joining in with the congregation on the final verse. I don't know how else to explain it. Instantly the understanding came to me that the additional voices I was hearing were those of spirits who were ancestors or future progeny of members in that area. I sensed that there was light all around us.

In the second conference session, which was held Sunday afternoon, the same phenomenon occurred at the exact same line of the song. Without even thinking about what had happened earlier in the day, the sound again transitioned during the third verse into something fuller and much more sublime. The additional voices seemed to be coming from beyond the congregation. Again, my emotions overcame me and I could do little more than mouth the words. I looked to my right and left and then behind me to see from where all of these additional voices were emanating but saw no one behind me singing except for the stake presidency and a couple of other conference speakers.

I felt very humbled that a heavenly choir may have helped deliver my final message to those among the congregation who had listening ears. The splendor of the voices, along with the very strong Spirit I felt while leading the music during the first and second sessions, led me to believe that perhaps this effort had met with some divine approval. I was certainly touched and continue to ponder this experience.

Final Farewells

"We traditionally hosted departing missionaries at the mission home the evening prior to their departure. As the end of our own mission approached, we met with our final group. After dinner and exit interviews, we gathered in a circle for one last meeting in which I invited each missionary to share a mission experience with the others.

Each of the ten missionaries spoke in turn. One of the sister missionaries remarked that "we, as Latter-day Saints, don't realize the tremendous power that has been given to us as God's children." She then went on to relate the importance of this power in missionary work.

While she was speaking, I noticed how the eyes of the other missionaries were transfixed on her countenance. One of the elders asked to speak with me just afterward in my office. He then related to me, in a very excited way, how that when the sister missionary began speaking of power, he could see light emanating from her body and head, extending outwards perhaps a foot or more, and especially from her head and face. He said the quality of light was splendidly white, and was apparent even against the backdrop of the muted white walls that were behind her. As he gazed around the room, he was stunned to see white light emanating from each of the other missionaries. He used his hands and arms to describe the transcendent scene—gesturing to depict a shape akin to a horizon of many rounded, connected mountains of light, demonstrating how the profile of shapes of the missionaries was imbued with a conjoined, flowing light, extending upward and outward by about one foot. Then he described that as the missionaries would move their arms or heads, the light would move right along with their bodies, encircling even their arms with a heavenly ring. He said he had never seen anything like it before! I assured him that others in the mission had been similarly privileged at times, and to regard his experience as a special gift from God.

Two days later, I met the aforementioned sister missionary again as she was departing with her parents, who had come to travel back home with her. I related to her what the elder had seen when she was speaking. She replied, "President, didn't you also see that light around everybody?" (I didn't.) She related that she, too, had seen the light emanating from everybody else during the meeting. She described the light very similarly to the elder and added one precious detail—that the light continued for a long time.

I thought it was very fitting that the particular sister missionary had been speaking when this "light fest" began, as she was a source or catalyst of much light for many of us. I am very humbled that we have missionaries with these spiritual gifts, and I am touched by the condescension of our God who would honor His servants with such a celestial imprimatur.

Missionary Letters

The final story recounted here comes from Elder Manfré, who wrote about something he observed while I was reading a few letters during one of our last zone conferences. Toward the latter part of our mission, I would begin the periodic zone meetings by reading excerpts from a handful of the missionaries' letters to me. The letters were read without me giving any identifying information about the sender, including the region from which the letters were sent, or when they were received. Elder Manfré's translated letter proceeds below.

"President, I had an interesting experience at the last conference. You know how usually, at the beginning of a [zone] conference and prior to your main talk, you often give announcements and relate things that are happening in our mission . . . and then you typically finish off that segment by reading some missionary experiences from the letters that you receive from missionaries?

"Well, during the conference this month, as you began reaching for the small group of letters that you had brought to share with us, your right arm, all the way down to your fingertips, was bright white. As you would read them and place them down at the side of the podium, that light remained perceptible in your right arm and in your hand. Finally, when you finished the last of these letters and reverently set it down on the pile with the rest of those letters, I saw this light gradually leave your arm, and then your hand, as it lifted off the stack of sacred missionary letters. I was in awe that, in some way, the Lord was showing me His respect for those letters and indicating to me their validity through this experience!"

To me, the message of his letter is both touching and powerful because it seems to confirm what I felt—that these missionary letters are sacred. I have felt impelled to compile a sampling of them, along with certain accounts from their journals and interviews, to share with a wider audience than just our mission. I humbly submit these records in hopes that your faith in the Lord Jesus Christ and your appreciation of His active ministry will increase.

About the Author

Dr. Babbel is Emeritus Professor of Insurance and Finance at The Wharton School of the University of Pennsylvania, having previously served as a finance and international business professor at the University of California at Berkeley. With over one hundred and thirty scholarly articles and publications to his credit, along with a number of books and monographs, his research has won national and international awards of distinction. He has lectured on five continents and advised country leaders at the highest levels. An accomplished biographical profile listee in Marquis *Who's Who in the World* and in *Who's Who in America* since 1992, Dr. Babbel received the Albert Nelson Marquis Lifetime Achievement Award in 2018. He presided with his wife over the Brasília Mission from 2002 to 2005.

Scan to visit

www.davebabbel.net

JOSÉ SMITH

— *la jornada de* —

UN PROFETA

SUSAN EVANS MCCLOUD

TRADUCIDO POR:
Catherine McCloud de Gonzalez and Jeannine George

EDITADO POR:
Darío C. Agüero

CFI
An imprint of Cedar Fort, Inc.
Springville, Utah

Obras Adicionales de
Susan Evans McCloud

Recientes

Stories of Lucy Mack Smith: Mother of the Restoration

Columnista de MormonTimes.com Escritora y creadora de la serie "Poets of the Restoration" para radio.lds.org

Escritora de "History of the Hymns," radio.lds.org

Escritora de dos importantes programas corales

Escritora de "A Celebration of Family History," abril de 2010

Misterio

Who Goes There?
Murder by the Sea
The Last Suspect
Storm & Deceit

Biografías

Stories of Lucy Mack Smith: Mother of the Restoration
Brigham Young, A Personal Portrait
Joseph Smith, a Photobiography
Not in Vain: the Story of Dr. Ellis Reynolds Shipp
The Best of Brigham Young: Over 300 Quotes & Sayings.

Teatro

Adaptación del libro
Charlie's Monument

Poesía

Songs of Life, 1985

Niños

Serie Mormon Girls, seis libros publicados en los noventa
Pioneer Stories of Faith and Courage
Black Stars Over Mexico
A. A. Seagull: Story of the Crickets and the Gulls (traducido al alemán)
I'm Going to Be Baptized

Otros

LDS Bride's Planner, 2002
Divine Nature: Mother's Quote Book

Letras

Himnos: "Señor, yo te seguiré" y "As Zion's Youth," publicados en *Hymns*, 1985 LDS hymnal

This Is My Day
(canción principal para álbum comercial)

Cry to the Wind
(canción principal para película comercial)

Mas de 20 canciones para cursos de estudio de seminario de la Iglesia de Jesucristo SUD en varias series "Quest," "Like unto Us," "Gates of Zion," "Not of the World"